How to Think Your Way to the Life You Want

A Guide to Understanding How Your Thoughts and Beliefs Create Your Life

How to Think
Your Way to the
Life You Want

A Guide to Understanding How Your
Thoughts and Beliefs Create Your Life

BRUCE I. DOYLE III, PH.D.

Cover design and art by Jessica Dacher
Text design and illustrations by ContentWorks, Inc.

Hampton Roads Publishing Company, Inc.
Charlottesville, VA 22906
www.hrpub.com

Library of Congress Cataloging-in-Publication Data available upon
request

ISBN: 978-1-57174-640-5

10 9 8 7 6 5 4 3 2 1

Printed on acid-free paper in Canada
TCP

To my daughters, Ellen and Megan,
and my grandchildren, Olivia, Zach, Lucy, and Brooke.
You light up my life!

It was one of those mornings—a cloud
hid the sun, looking up, the bear said,
"Oh, this is no fun!"

So she started to think about fields full
of flowers and bright, shining rainbows
that follow the showers.

Then she smiled a big smile for she
knew suddenly, a day is as nice as you
think it to be.

Contents

Preface

What I am about to share with you comes straight from the heart. It's about what I have experienced and what is true for me. I offer no scientific proof for any of my comments. Most of my analogies are simple, in an attempt to illustrate what—scientifically—must be beyond human comprehension. They are presented only to give you something to which you can relate.

If what I have to say inspires you to want to know more, I have accomplished my mission: to spread the word that we are all unlimited beings and only our individual beliefs hold us back. Our beliefs originate from those thoughts that we have accepted as true. Every one of our thoughts is a thread in the fabric of what we experience as our lives. And each one of us weaves our own cloth. Collectively, we weave the tapestry of Life—which *all* experience.

If the life you are experiencing isn't fulfilling, my hope is that by understanding the "fundamentals of thought," you will gain new insights into achieving the life you deserve—one that has no limits.

Acknowledgments

Thanks to each individual who has ever played a role in my life. I now know that you were there to reflect back to me my own projections and beliefs about myself. I finally got it. For those of you whom I blamed—please forgive me. To those who inspired me—I bow.

Many thanks to Marjorie McLaughlin for her support in conducting my Power-Up for Success workshops, for proofreading my doctoral dissertation, and for editing my published articles.

Many thanks also to Sydne Heather Schinkel, author of *Earthbridge Crossing*, and to her husband, Thomas, for their professional contribution to my previous book, *Before You Think Another Thought*.

Special thanks to Sharron Barron of Finally Unlimited for providing the "we's" teachings—my introduction to belief systems.

Special thanks also to Harry Palmer for creating the Avatar Course. Avatar gave me a deeper understanding of belief systems and provided me with additional tools for moving closer to experiencing unlimited living.

And finally, heartfelt thanks to the part of me that now has the courage to share things with you—about myself—that a short time ago would have been unthinkable. May my sharing be helpful.

Love and appreciation to all.

Introduction

Have you ever had the feeling that you were like a small canoe floating in the ocean—solely at the whim of the overpowering waves? No matter how hard you paddled, you could make no impact on your course; you felt totally out of control.

With all the books, tapes, workshops, and seminars available on various aspects of personal development—from basic attitude adjustment to spiritual enlightenment—there still seem to be a great many people on the planet with this out-of-control feeling, trying desperately to gain control over their lives. You may be one of them. Self-esteem for many is at an all-time low. What's going on? What's missing?

What's missing is a clear understanding of the fundamentals of how each of us creates our own life experiences. Yes, I said our *own*. We are all responsible for our own experiences.

Thoughts and beliefs are the basic elements of all creation. They exist as tiny waves of energy called thoughtforms, whose sole purpose is to carry out the intent of the thinker.

By understanding how your thoughts and beliefs operate, you will be able to see how some of the limiting beliefs that you hold keep you from achieving your goals. These beliefs can be removed.

Understanding that you have an *energetic signature,* which is derived from your beliefs, will help you understand how you attract certain events, circumstances, and relationships into your life. By changing your beliefs, you will attract new, more desirable experiences.

When you realize that your thoughts and beliefs determine what you experience, you're on your way to having mastery over your life.

How Thoughts Work

Thought

Did you ever have thoughts that you didn't want to share? Thoughts about other people that you knew would upset them if you verbalized them? Maybe about their clothes, manners, or things they did that bothered you. You hesitated to share your thoughts because you wanted to maintain peace in the relationship. You may have even berated yourself for having such awful thoughts—"How could I think such a thing?"

Most people consider thoughts as ideas or notions that reside in their heads for their own private use. Thoughts help you to figure out things, evaluate situations, make decisions, and generate feelings, and sometimes they seem to drive you crazy (well, almost).

Thoughts or ideas may seem to reside in your head, but, in reality, each thought exists as a minute wave of energy called a thoughtform. A thoughtform is real—it exists. It happens to not be noticed by you because its energy vibration (frequency) is outside the range of human senses. It operates faster than the speed of light and is, therefore, not visible to you.

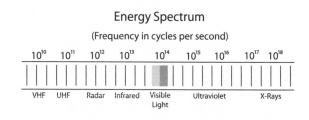

Energy Spectrum

(Frequency in cycles per second)

| 10^{10} | 10^{11} | 10^{12} | 10^{13} | 10^{14} | 10^{15} | 10^{16} | 10^{17} | 10^{18} |

| VHF | UHF | Radar | Infrared | Visible Light | Ultraviolet | X-Rays |

Our senses are limited to a specific range of frequencies.

It might be helpful for you to understand this concept by relating it to something you already know, but which you

How to Think Your Way to the Life You Want

probably have not given much thought. If you're like most of us, you have a favorite radio station. Perhaps an FM station for listening to "your kind" of music. Let's say it's 102.7 on the dial.

What that number means is that the frequency of transmission for that station is 102.7 megahertz (mega-cycles). *Mega* is the metric designation for one million. The energy transmitted by the station vibrates continuously in the space around you. But unless your radio is tuned to the frequency of 102.7 million cycles per second, you are unaware of it.

My point is this: There is a lot of information vibrating in the space around us that we are not aware of because our senses are limited to a specific range of frequencies. And some of the information vibrating in the space is in the form of tiny, subtle thoughtforms.

The mission of each thoughtform is to fulfill the intent of the thought—to carry out the thinker's desires or intentions. It does so by attracting to it similar thoughtforms to help it fulfill itself. In effect, you are like a radio station, WYOU, broadcasting your desires, intentions, and ideas out into the universe—completely uncensored. Picture a king who sends selected members of his court out into his kingdom to fulfill his desires (even his secret ones).

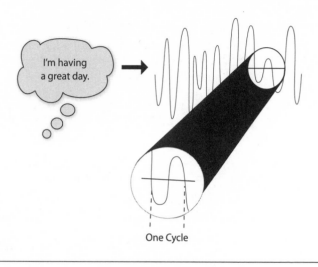

One Cycle

Thoughts exist as thoughtforms.

Have you ever had someone say to you, "Watch what you wish for; you're liable to get it"? Have you ever had the same thought, at exactly the same time, as someone close to you? Have people ever accused you of reading their minds? Are there people in your life that you feel "tuned in" to? Some individuals are very sensitive to picking up thought-form vibrations. If you answered yes to any of these questions, you are probably one of them.

Beliefs

Thoughts that you accept as true become your beliefs. Together, all your individual beliefs make up your belief system.

If I told you that the moon is made of swiss cheese, I doubt that you would believe me. Based on what you already know, you wouldn't consider it to be true, and it would not become part of your belief system. But if I said, "The weather patterns around the world are going to continue to change dramatically," you would probably agree. Some of you have real tangible evidence of this already. You would feel that my statement is true and add it to your already-existing beliefs.

Beliefs are specialized thoughtforms that become part of your individual belief system. Furthermore, existing as waves of energy that you radiate out into the universe, they accumulate similar thoughtforms in order to create events, circumstances, and relationships that substantiate your beliefs.

"Wait a minute," you say. "Don't you have that backward? I experience something, then I can believe it. You know the old saying, 'I'll believe it when I see it.'"

Yes, that is a very old saying, but in reality, it happens the other way around. You will experience something only if you believe it. The belief must come first. If you experienced something that you didn't believe, how could you believe it?

Your experience confirms your belief—belief precedes experience. It's the way the universe works.

If you believe that you're poor, can you experience being rich? If you believe that you're fat, can you experience being thin? If you believe that you're dumb, can you experience being smart? Think about it! What you believe is what you experience.

Beliefs are usually described as either conscious beliefs or subconscious beliefs.

Conscious beliefs are those that you are aware of; with some prompting, you could write down a few. Conscious beliefs can be empowering—such as "I'm smart" and "Life's exciting"—or limiting, such as "I'm clumsy" and "Men hate me."

Subconscious beliefs are beliefs that you are not aware of. You are unaware that they exist, and the experiences they create for you are seen as "That's the way life is." You have no sense of responsibility for having accepted them as beliefs. The beliefs are transparent to you.

An example of a limiting subconscious belief might be "I can never have things my way," stemming from a childhood decision about authority. This belief could show up as repeated conflicts with bosses later in life. Such a person might frequently say, "All bosses are jerks," not realizing that he is operating out of a transparent belief. As you know, not all people experience their bosses that way.

An example of an empowering subconscious belief might be something like "I'm always safe." People with this belief might not be aware of it, yet they live their lives having no fear for their safety. They would simply not attract a potentially harmful situation and would see no threat to themselves even if one arose.

Beliefs

		Empowering	Limiting
Mind	Conscious	• I'm smart • Things work out for me • I'm healthy • Life's exciting	• I'm not very smart • I can't . . . • I'll always be fat • Men hate me
	Subconscious	• The world is safe • I'll be taken care of • I belong • I'm okay	• I'm a failure • Nobody loves me • I don't deserve happiness • The world is scary

In my belief model, you can see that there are basically four areas of beliefs that can be considered. At the conscious and the subconscious levels, you have both empowering and limiting beliefs. It's the limiting beliefs that we'll discuss in more detail. After you eliminate these beliefs, you will expend less energy and attention creating the circumstances that you choose to have in your life.

Every thought and every belief has its corresponding thoughtform, which is a dynamic wave of energy that has two key parameters: a frequency of vibration corresponding to its intent and a magnitude corresponding to the amount of desire associated with it. Each of our belief systems can be represented by an energetic signature (not unlike our personalized signature) that is unique to us and essentially defines us. We are all like energetic magnets drawing our experiences to us.

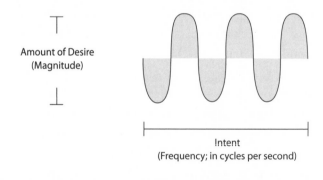

Every thoughtform has two key parameters.

Have you ever noticed that, when you meet them for the first time, you feel comfortable with some people and you don't feel comfortable with others? You're sensing their energy fields. The ones with whom you feel comfortable will most likely have similar beliefs. Trust your feelings.

When you are in close relationships with people, you can feel that they are upset before they say a word. You can sense that their energy has shifted—to a lower frequency.

Your basic energy signature is the sum of all your thoughts and beliefs. You define your personality, physical attributes, and behavior. You are the only one who can create or change your thoughts and your beliefs. And your beliefs create what you experience as life.

Have you ever tried to change someone else? Didn't work, did it? No one can change someone else's thoughts. Individuals must want to change and do so on their own. Consequently, if each of us is responsible for our own thoughts, we are likewise responsible for our own feelings. Your feelings are generated by your thoughts. Notice that when you have positive thoughts, you feel good. When you think negative thoughts, how do you feel?

Have you ever been accused of hurting others' feelings? When you realize that you can't create their thoughts, you likewise understand that you can't create their feelings. How freeing! Now you can let go of the old belief that we all grew up with: "You shouldn't hurt other people's feelings."

Naturally, there is appropriateness in all things. But you can't determine others' feelings; their feelings are strictly theirs.

My daughter Megan's college psychology text had an example of a man who was severely bumped from behind on a crowded subway. His immediate reaction was raw anger, the source of which is his visualization of a large robust woman bullying her way through the crowd. As he turned to confront her, he realized that the person who bumped him was blind. His feelings immediately shifted as his mind filled with thoughts of compassion. His thoughts, his feelings.

Do you remember your experience—how you felt—when you believed in Santa Claus? Quite exciting, wasn't it? What was your experience when you found out that he really didn't exist, and you changed your belief? Took a lot of fun out of your life, didn't it? Different belief, different experience!

Beliefs

↓

Thoughts

↓

Feelings

↓

Reactions

Shared beliefs can extend to many individuals. The different religions operating on the planet are examples of many individuals sharing common beliefs. All the various social, financial, and political structures around the globe are also examples of belief systems. The important thing to remember is that each individual has the right to his or her own experiences and, consequently, to his or her own beliefs.

It's when you try to convince others that your beliefs are the only truth that difficulty arises. You see, we all have our own truths. Truth belongs to the believer. There are as many truths as there are believers. Many can share common beliefs, but essentially each of us creates our own unique perspective of the world based on our beliefs.

In essence then, each of us lives in and is responsible for our own world. Certainly your world is different than mine and, likewise, that of your neighbors. Did you ever wonder how you appear to someone else? Did you ever wonder what it was like to walk in someone else's shoes? We all see life from our own perspectives (based on our beliefs), and for each person, it's different. In fact, the only real difference in any of us is what we believe. Sure, many of us look different, but maybe that's also a belief.

If you find yourself trying to convince someone about something you believe, ask yourself if you really believe it. Needing to convince someone else about your truth would imply that you doubt your own belief. When you really believe something, there is no doubt. Hoping it might be true would allow for doubt. When you have no doubt, you can stand in the face of any challenge unshaken and without emotion—you know the truth.

Thoughtform Structure

Understanding the structure of thoughtforms will greatly assist you in understanding their impact on belief systems.

In my view, thoughtforms tend to come in clusters, much like clumps of grapes. Take a clump of grapes, pull off the grapes, and you have an array of branches going off in all directions. As you go back toward the main branch, the branches get thicker and stronger. You end up with the core branch.

In my analogy, the core branch equates to the root thoughtform—the initial and deep-rooted thoughtform that is the primary cause of the issue involved. With any new idea, issue, or situation, the initial thoughtform that you generate establishes the basic pattern, or blueprint, of experience. Subsequent thoughts and beliefs relating to that subject will attach themselves to the root thoughtform like branches in a cluster. To clear out an issue, you have to pull the original thoughtform out by the roots.

A former colleague of mine, whenever he encounters something new, usually says, "This is going to be hard." Guess what he experiences? His life is a series of struggles that require a lot of his effort to overcome.

The strongest and most influential limiting beliefs with which you will have to deal will probably be about your self-concept (your beliefs about how you see yourself), your "I am" statements. These beliefs usually originate in infancy and/or childhood. They are often referred to as *conditioning* or *programming.* I will not use either of these terms. To me, they imply that something was done to you—an implication that tends to generate blame and avoid self-responsibility. No one other than the believer—you—can accept or choose a belief.

So even as an infant, you did the choosing. Since the experience probably involved a caretaker or someone in an influential position, you naturally accepted that person's assessment. What reason did you have to doubt their assessment of you? None.

But now, as an adult, you can reevaluate your decision to see if you still wish to hold specific beliefs that are no longer in your best interest. Beliefs are like ideas—good ones you keep, limiting ones you discard.

An Empowering Example

Let's look at the favorable impact of an empowering belief first.

Jane, as a small child, had a very positive environment. She was loved by her parents, siblings, and friends. She was encouraged to try things and was supported and given praise.

She adopted the belief, "I always have everything I need, and I am secure."

That basic belief, in order to fulfill itself, acted to positively influence every major facet of her life. Throughout her life, unless impacted by a conflicting belief, she experienced that belief. As an adult, she saw its effect in her work—a fulfilling job. Her finances continually sustained her needs. Her relationships were satisfying and stable and provided her with the love that she deserved. That strong empowering belief provided a very supportive root for her life's experiences.

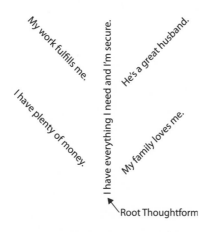

Jane's thoughtform structure

A Limiting Example

Jim, on the other hand, was not as fortunate. Jim's environment stemmed from a marriage that was not planned. His father married his mother because he thought doing so was his duty, but he resented Jim for having been born. He paid little attention to Jim except to criticize or severely discipline him. Fortunately, Jim's mother was caring and loved him dearly. But her affection for him only angered his jealous father.

Out of all of this, Jim soon decided (created the belief) that it was his fault that his parents were unhappy. This thought translated into, "I'm responsible for others' unhappiness." Can you see how that root belief would negatively impact every major area of Jim's life? What a burden to feel responsible for other people's unhappiness—a life of trying to please others.

How would Jim, as an adult, negotiate a deal or ask for a raise if he thought the other person might get upset? Can you imagine Jim trying to please his mate all of the time? How would it feel to Jim if someone around him were not happy? He would always feel like it was his fault. Life for Jim would mean no emotional freedom for himself; he would always be monitoring his behavior. That's what a limiting belief does. And to Jim, his behavior would feel normal. The limitation would be transparent to him.

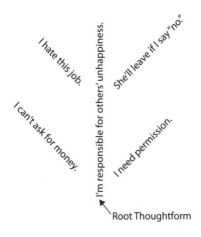

Jim's thoughtform structure

Again, remember that there is no blame for Jim's father; it was Jim who decided to accept what he believed about himself. At the time, that belief may have made a lot of sense. A very strong limiting factor in the blueprint for determining Jim's life experience was put in place by what might appear to be a simple, harmless belief.

Life Incidents

Once a root thoughtform is established, incidents will occur to continue to provide evidence to the believer that the belief is true. Let's try another example to further illustrate the point.

Sally's mother had to attend an unexpected business meeting during a time when her regular sitter was not available. After several phone calls, her mother was finally able to reach a neighbor, who agreed to look after the child. The neighbor was a nice lady, but she was not used to being around four-year-old children.

Sally sensed her awkwardness. She didn't feel at all comfortable with the new sitter and started to cry. The sitter, trying to get her to stop, began a series of make-believe games that involved making strange faces. This just added to Sally's fear, and she cried harder. The sitter, in sheer frustration, picked up Sally, took her into her bedroom, and plopped her on the bed. As the sitter slammed the door behind her, she hollered, "You're the worst kid I've ever seen." Sally, in that moment of vulnerability, decided, "There's something wrong with me."

As Sally grew older, incidents occurred and similar thoughtforms were created to fulfill the intent of the core belief, "There's something wrong with me." These similar thoughtforms attached to the root thoughtform like the branches of the grape cluster we discussed. All areas of her life became affected by this very basic core belief—of which, by the way, she was totally unaware.

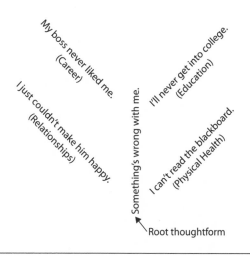

My boss never liked me. (Career)

I just couldn't make him happy. (Relationships)

I'll never get into college. (Education)

I can't read the blackboard. (Physical Health)

Something's wrong with me.

↖ Root thoughtform

Sally's thoughtform structure

The following figure contains some examples of real-life situations that could stem from an early belief that "there is something wrong with me." The related beliefs about poor eyesight at six years of age, difficulty with academics in the teens, work issues at age thirty, and a relationship issue at age forty could all develop from the one, simple, limiting belief, "There's something wrong with me."

Naturally, these same situations could be generated from other belief sources. If you relate to one of these conditions, don't assume your belief is also "There's something wrong

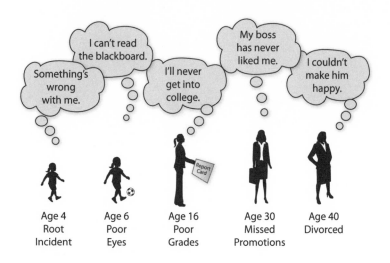

with me." Do some exploring: Can you see repeated patterns of experience in the lives of those close to you? What about yourself? Do you keep having a recurring experience? What belief might be behind these situations?

Self-Sabotage

Frequently, people experience unexplained behavior that some would describe as self-sabotage. It's like having in your subconscious mind a little gremlin who is very mischievous. Every once in a while, he does something odd—usually at an inappropriate time—over which you seem to have no control. At least that's the way it appears. It's that misplaced comment during an important meeting that just kills the opportunity you were counting on. You walk out of the meeting muttering to yourself, "Why in the world did I say that?"

Maybe that little gremlin doesn't exist. Consider the existence of a limiting thoughtform for which you are totally responsible, but of which you are not aware. What do you think might happen to someone in an interview who believed "I just don't do well in interviews"? That person would probably say something unintended at the most inappropriate time. It might be called self-sabotage, but, more than likely, there is a limiting belief at work.

What I'm talking about seems subtle, but can you see the significant impact that these limiting beliefs have on your life? Here's a real-life example.

Several years ago, I was working with a client—I'll call him Pete—who was conducting a nationwide job search. We spent many hours together, mostly with me just listening and observing his frustration. Pete was having a difficult time making a decision about what he wanted to do. It seemed that every day he was excited about something new and was off in a different direction.

I had introduced my concepts about belief systems to Pete, and he had an intellectual understanding of what I was saying, but no real, major "aha" yet. As Pete and I worked more closely together, I began to make notes of the limiting beliefs that I frequently heard him say. The beliefs I heard most often were:

"There is a price to pay for everything."

"It's not possible to have it all."

"Nothing is what people perceive it to be."

Pete and I discussed these frequently expressed beliefs, and it was clear that even though he had an intellectual idea of the concept "beliefs determine experience," he hadn't internalized it. He was totally unaware that these beliefs were operating. He was so used to his mode of operation that it had become transparent to him.

Once we discussed these limiting beliefs openly, he was able to get in touch with them. He had grown up with them—they were the same as his father's.

Can you see how someone operating with these beliefs would have a difficult time making a decision? He was setting himself up. There was only one right decision for him to make, and he had better make the right choice, or he would have hell to pay.

A few days after our discussion, Pete came into my office to tell me that he had shared his new insight with his Realtor. He was relating his belief to her that "things aren't what they seem," when she replied, "You're right! All my clients have hidden agendas." Without hesitation, Pete declared, "And she has been a Realtor for ten years!"

Pete was still looking for evidence to prove that his belief was true—for everyone.

After I pointed out that his friend was merely attracting the clients who would substantiate her belief, he began to see my point. He was becoming more aware and could begin the process of sorting out those beliefs that were getting in his way.

Attention

What you put your attention on strengthens or expands in your life.

Scientists are discovering more and more evidence that we humans are not independent observers of a mechanical universe. Our attention, backed by the intent of our beliefs, creates what we experience as our lives. Scientifically, one might say that focusing your attention on the energy field of consciousness, which contains the waves of all possibilities, creates the particles (events and materializations) that you experience as your reality.

This is a very important concept. Let me repeat it: what you put your attention on strengthens or expands in your life. This one idea alone can make a big difference for you.

Remember the last time you were considering buying a new car? You had your attention focused on it, and what happened? All of a sudden, you noticed many different types, models, and colors of cars, "for sale" signs in windows, ads in the paper, and people relaying information to you about a friend who was thinking of selling his car. Your attention brought things into your awareness because of your focus. The moment you purchased your new car, your attention shifted. The same information about cars was available, but it was no longer attracted to your awareness. Your attention was focused elsewhere.

Imagine a coal miner with a helmet that contains a light to enable him to see directly in front of him. Now picture yourself with a similar light beaming from your forehead. Think of it as your attention beam. How often are you aware of where it's focused?

It is important to focus your attention effectively. In other words, don't waste your creative energy. Without deliberate focus, you're spreading your attention around randomly, achieving no real benefit for yourself. Keep your attention focused on something positive, and good things begin to happen.

This is the real reason for goal setting. It's the mental focus that helps you achieve your goals. Your focus is actually strengthening the thoughtform that you have expressed as your goal. Unfortunately, many of us have been oriented to the pass-fail aspect of goal setting, and so, to avoid failure, we don't set goals. Yes, the concept of pass-fail is a belief—a very strong shared one.

If there is something in your life that you want, keep your attention focused on that goal. If things show up—and they will—that seem to get in the way, don't focus on them. Handle them, but stay focused on your goal. It's when you focus on the obstacles that you tend to give up. Think about what we have already discussed. What happens when you focus on the obstacles? Right—your focus just strengthens the thoughtforms related to the obstacle. Stay focused on the goal.

You might have a goal that you believe can be achieved only if you have a certain amount of money. Instead of focusing on the goal, you focus on the fact that you don't have enough money. What gets strengthened is the thoughtform for not having enough money. Maybe there is a way to achieve the goal without money. By not focusing on the goal, you restrict possibilities, of which you may not be aware, from occurring.

Victoria Heasley, a massage therapist, constantly amazes me with how she obtains what she needs. She is the kind of person who says to herself, "I sure could use another couch," and within days a friend who is moving out of town calls her to ask if she knows anyone who could use a good couch. If she focused on worrying about the money to buy a couch, she would miss these opportunities. Stay focused on your goal!

Remember the story about the little steam engine who believed he could make it up the mountain. He was really focused on his goal. How well do you think he would have done chanting, "I'll never make it. My joints are sore. I'll never make it. My joints are sore"?

Knowing where your attention is focused is also important because you physically experience what you focus your attention on. You're probably focused on limiting or negative thoughts any time you are experiencing something unpleasant. So if you want to change how you feel, shift your attention to something else—a pleasant memory, a different subject, anything. Or, best of all, become an observer of your thoughts and just watch them float by. This can be quite relaxing and can be referred to as meditating. By monitoring where you are focusing your attention, you will begin to gain insight into why you are experiencing what you are experiencing.

As you read through this book, notice your emotions. If you detect uncomfortable ones, see if you can determine what belief is being challenged by what you're reading at that moment. Fear, worry, and doubt are probably the three strongest thoughtforms on the planet. They will rob you of all your desires. If you can get in touch with and remove the limiting beliefs behind these culprits, you'll be a new person.

What You Believe
Is What You Get

Self-Responsibility

The fact that you create all your life experiences is a rude awakening for most people. You may be sitting there right now doubting every word that I'm saying. And that's OK. All I ask is that you consider what's being said. Give it some thought. Be open to the possibility that it's worth exploring.

The good news is that with the recognition that you are creating your life (and some forgiveness thrown in), you can start taking charge—as the designer of your life, no longer a victim of life's random circumstances. You become self-responsible.

Knowing you are responsible for your experiences, and always have been, gives you the opportunity to start creating the experiences you would like to have, rather than experiencing life by default. A great deal of personal power is available to you—much more than you've imagined. By personal power, I'm not talking about the kind of power that you have over others. I'm talking about inner power—the power of self-confidence and self-esteem. When you have that kind of power, there is no need or desire to have power over anyone or anything else.

I sometimes reflect on my earlier years as a young manager in the corporate world. A few of our senior executives appeared, to me, to need power—the power-over-others type. It seemed that they wasted a lot of time and talent (theirs) in business-review sessions intimidating our management team. They were good at generating fear and stimulating feelings of inadequacy. It's a shame some of them didn't have the personal power to act more like coaches. I'm sure that my peers, and the business, and I would have been better off.

It's nice to look back and see the situation from a new perspective. It feels good to know that their beliefs created their experiences and my beliefs created mine. This takes away all the blame. What else would some young manager attract to himself if he had the subconscious limiting belief,

"It's always my fault"? I was constantly putting myself in situations where I had to defend myself, trying to prove that it wasn't my fault. Not a comfortable position to be in. But that's how limiting thoughtforms work. I'm sure glad that this one has been resolved. As you begin to experience the power of changing your beliefs, your desire to know more and more about it becomes compelling.

The Mirror

When we examine a little further the concept that your beliefs determine your experiences, we will see that your experiences (external events) are driven by your beliefs (internal events). You can then use the outer events to see what you really believe. This is often referred to as mirroring.

The universe you experience mirrors your belief system back to you. If you want to change your experiences, you must change your beliefs. Your life experiences are great teachers, but if you don't realize that you're in class, you may miss the entire course. Sure, it will be offered again, but you know what happens to tuition every year!

As you work your way through the ideas in this book, it would be helpful if you started making a list of the situations,

The universe mirrors your beliefs.

circumstances, or people that give you unpleasant feelings, as they come to mind. These notes will give you a starting point as you explore later what your mirror has in store for you. Also, consider someone you know very well and jot down what that person might believe in order to be having the experiences he or she is having. What about you? Are there some experiences in your life that you would prefer not to have? What beliefs might you hold that are creating these experiences?

In most cases, the reflections of unpleasantness that are mirrored back to you (your perceptions) have to do with beliefs you hold about yourself. Poor self-esteem is the major cause of individuals' dissatisfaction with their lives. We experience our defined inadequacies and limiting beliefs (many of which are transparent) by seeing in others what we are not seeing or what we refuse to accept about ourselves. Next time you feel critical of someone, reflect back and see if you aren't, in some way, identifying with a trait in yourself that you don't like or haven't accepted.

If you issue a judgment—either verbally or mentally—about someone else's behavior and that judgment is accompanied by emotion, you're getting hooked. The emotion is a great indicator that you have an opportunity for some self-discovery and possible healing on the issue in question. If you only observe someone else's behavior, just notice it without any emotional response, you are clear.

Judgments are tied to beliefs.

Don't be alarmed if you find yourself issuing judgments. This behavior is something that may take some time to change, should you choose to do so. Every one of those judgments is tied to a belief. It may take a while to track down all those beliefs. Be kind to yourself as you do so. Judging yourself for judging others just compounds the issue.

I can recall often hearing, as I was growing up, my grandfather and my dad speak critically and very judgmentally of other people—those who were different from them. Those of another race and people who were poor were deemed "naturally lazy," and those who were "the filthy rich" were "crooks." I didn't think that much of those opinions rubbed off; we had only one black person in school, and I liked him a lot. He was always in a good mood and usually had us in stitches. Later in life I had other friends who were different from me.

I never thought, therefore, that I had an issue with race until I fell in love, head over heels, with the woman of my dreams. Shortly after we began dating, she informed me that her previous relationship had been with a black man. I was stunned. My judgment was put right in my face. It wasn't transparent any longer. I had a long list of judgmental beliefs about the kind of white women who would date a black man. I had to either walk away from the relationship to prove that

I was right or look at my limiting beliefs. They sure didn't fit my current beliefs about the woman I was dating. The mental conflict was agonizing.

Fortunately, she was understanding, and I was able to get in touch with my limiting beliefs about the situation and release them. It took several tough months of soul-searching to let go of them—not to mention the male insecurity issues they dug up.

Things always happen for a good reason. Several years later, my youngest daughter introduced us to her new boyfriend during parents' weekend at college. You guessed it—he was black. I was pleased that it didn't bother me a bit. He was a nice young man. It felt good to have that issue behind me, too.

Each time you let go of a limiting belief, life gets calmer and calmer. The mental chatter just diminishes. It's your assessment (perception) of external events that creates your experience of them. If you don't like what you're experiencing, you can always revise your assessment of what's happening.

Positive Attitude

With your new understanding of energetic vibrations, thoughtforms, and focus of attention, you should see clearly now why so much emphasis is placed on having a positive attitude or positive beliefs. Positive beliefs create positive thoughtforms, which attract positive events and circumstances into your life.

I used to think having a positive attitude was something that each of us should have to be more acceptable. That may be true, but the real impact of being positive has to do with your state of being—your vibrational state—and what it will attract to you.

People who just pretend to have a positive attitude may be more acceptable, but they will still attract according to how they are really vibrating; the energy they are emanating will attract their circumstances. So the message is clear. With your new insight into the fundamentals of thought, you'll want to start immediately making sure you're focused on being positive. Adopt the attitude that everything that happens in your life happens for a good reason. This will get you off to a great start.

Earlier in my career, during a business trip to Chicago, I was snowed in for three days in O'Hare International Airport. There were several feet of snow on the ground, and everything was at a standstill. During the second day, the restaurants began running out of food, stranded mothers were overwhelmed with crying children, and people were fed up with the whole situation, mostly from not knowing when it would end.

The range of attitudes that the situation evoked in people was amazing. I saw the worst, and I saw the best. Some travelers were downright nasty, greedy, and could think of nothing but themselves. I wondered what they must have been believing about their personal situations to be having such dreadful experiences. On the other hand, most of the people went out of their way to help others, especially those who had small children.

People's experiences of that situation were directly related to what they believed was happening. Next time you're involved in a trying situation, look around and see if you can think of what others might be believing to be having the experiences they are having. It's also revealing to include your own experience. What beliefs might be creating your experience?

I've learned a lot about positive attitude as I've studied more about thoughtforms and energetic attraction. I constantly see its validity. To remind myself to stay positive, I've created the phrase, "Everything works for me easily and effortlessly." It keeps me in a positive frame of mind, no matter what happens, so I can continue to emit positive energy and attract positive circumstances. Here's another true story.

For many years, I was fortunate to have never had a flat tire or a breakdown on the highway. Such inconveniences always occurred where they could be easily handled. That changed one day as I was on my way home from the office. The clutch in my sports car failed as I was pulling away from a stoplight. Luckily, no one was immediately behind me. My first thought was, "I wonder what the benefit of this is going to be."

After pushing the car to the side of the road, I walked across the street and called my auto-club emergency number. Within thirty minutes, the car was loaded on a flatbed truck, and we were on our way. The driver dropped me off at my house and delivered the car to the Porsche garage, Team Stuttgart. I was amazed at how smoothly everything went.

The next day, Dusty, my mechanic, called to tell me that a clip had come loose on the clutch cable—a very minor problem. Then he asked if I was interested in selling the car. I said that I was. He then informed me that while my car was in the shop, a gentlemen had come in looking for advice on where to buy a good used Porsche. The gentleman liked my 912E, and Dusty hoped that it was OK to have given him my phone number. I sold the car to that same gentleman a week later. Did my clutch cable break for a good reason? I guess it depends on what you believe.

Speaking of attitude, how would you describe your attitude about yourself? Is it positive? Yeah, I know, you can give me a long list of all the things you believe are wrong with you—your body's not perfect (according to whose standards?), you've done some terrible things (says who?), you're this, you're that. Fine, go ahead and make the list, and then, without judgment, just lovingly accept yourself. "Accept" doesn't mean anything but that—accept, with no judgments. "This is how I see me. I accept myself. It's OK to be me." Say it: "It's OK to be me." Great. Again: "It's OK to be me."

I'm fat
I'm not very smart
I don't make friends easily
I'm bashful
I smoke too much
I don't spend enough time with my children

Please note that your list of judgments about yourself (either written or mental) is a list of beliefs. Nothing more, nothing less. They can be changed. Remember, beliefs determine experience. You experience "you" as you have defined yourself. What you believe about yourself must be what you experience; otherwise, you wouldn't believe it. Yes, just like circumstances and events, your self-concept is yours—your own beliefs about yourself.

Earlier in my life, I had what many longed for—a good job, a big house, an attractive wife, and three young daughters whom I adored. But at a very deep level, a part of me wanted to be free, and I left a seventeen-year marriage. The guilt over destroying the lives of four people for whom I cared deeply altered how I saw myself.

During the next six years, the universe reflected back to me my deeply held (transparent) belief that I had done something very bad for which I deserved to be punished. My second marriage and several executive-level jobs ended in disappointment. Naturally, at the time, I had no idea that my beliefs were creating my experiences.

It was excerpts from an essay that my daughter Ellen wrote for application to college that finally gave me a new perspective on the situation. This positive point of view allowed me to start examining my false belief that I had damaged my daughters. I realized that my guilt was my own doing. I needed to see the situation in a new light. Today, all three girls have finished college and are creating successful lives for themselves.

My parents divorced the year I turned 13. At the time, I thought it was the greatest tragedy that could ever happen. But four years later, despite the sadness and confusion, it has provided me with some wonderful opportunities and experiences.

Traveling to visit my father in various locations, I have also had to be responsible for my younger sister. Our relationship has become very close because we have to depend on each other.

Because of my parents' divorce, I have had to become more independent at an earlier age than I might have otherwise had to do. I think learning to do lots of things myself rather than rely on others has helped me in my personal life and schoolwork

—Ellen Doyle, college application essay

Your acceptance of yourself, just as you are, is the first step in exploring the limiting beliefs you have about yourself. Acceptance removes the resistance to experiencing yourself as you are and helps keep your energy positive. It also frees up wasted energy so it can be used in accessing and changing those beliefs that you would like to change. Notice that I said "those beliefs that *you would like to change.*" You are free to believe what you wish. Change only what you wish to change. After all, it's your experience.

Experiencing

I've used the word *experiencing* a lot. What does experiencing really mean? Experiencing, as I am referring to it, is simply being in touch with what you are feeling. That's the only way you can truly experience anything—you must feel it! It sounds simple enough, but many of us don't allow ourselves to feel; consequently, we don't fully experience life.

Have you ever driven down the highway and suddenly realized that the past twenty miles went by without you noticing them? Why was that? Because you had your attention somewhere else. You missed experiencing (the feelings associated with) the beautiful countryside, the sunshine radiating off the autumn leaves, and the two deer grazing just behind the white picket fence. There is a difference between having the experience of a thirty-minute commute and fully experiencing the ride home from the office.

It was during a Hakomi Therapy training session a few years ago that I finally realized the difference. In Hakomi Therapy, the focus is on getting your clients in touch with what they are physically experiencing (feeling) in the present moment about a previous situation, rather than mentalizing (talking about) it. The term "being mindful" is used to describe the concept.

So to really experience anything fully, you must be mindful; you must place your attention on how you are feeling. Next time you're riding in the car, see if you can experience the trip a little differently.

Have you ever "tuned someone out" because you didn't want the experience (feeling) of being with or listening to them? Make sure you are not "tuning yourself out" of much of your life.

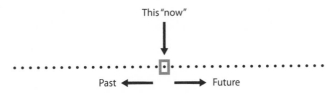

From time to time, we all try to communicate to others how we feel. Words such as *love, happy, joyful,* and *excited* are verbal symbols for expressing varying degrees of feeling good. *Bored, hate, sorrow,* and *mad* are symbols for feeling bad. And what you experience either feels good or it doesn't. No matter how each of us arrives at it, success for all of us is finding out what makes us feel good. And the only time to feel anything (experience it) is in the present moment—right *now.* Whoops! That *now* is already gone—gone forever.

The time line for life is really an infinite line of very short periods of *now,* the present moment. Periods of *now* that have already occurred we call history, or the past. We can no longer experience them. That's right! We can no longer experience them.

"But," you say, "I experience a lot of pain about things that happened in the past." That may be true, but you are not experiencing the past; you are experiencing your beliefs about the past. This is another one of those subtle distinctions that is quite profound. The same goes for the future. It's your story or beliefs—usually in the form of worry—that will cause unpleasant *nows* to occur. Isn't it amazing how easy it is to keep yourself from enjoying each successive now— life?

The importance of being consciously aware of your state during the present *now* has a lot to do with establishing your experience in future *nows.* If you are positive in this *now,* are deliberately focused on your desires for the future, and have no limiting beliefs about your ability to create your desires, you can count on your desires manifesting for you. Unfortunately, many of us have doubts about our abilities. These doubts are just beliefs, but they have a canceling effect on our ability to create. As I mentioned earlier, fear, worry, and doubt are the strongest limiting conditions for most of us.

Mary Burmeister, the founder of Jin Shin Jyutsu, Inc., says, "Worry is prayer for what you do not want" and "Fear is false evidence appearing real." Also, I heard somewhere that worry is like a rocking chair; it gives you something to do, but it doesn't get you anywhere. When you can remove the limiting beliefs behind fear, worry, and doubt, your life will begin to flow more smoothly.

Why You're Not Getting What You Want

By now it should be clear that what keeps you from realizing your full potential or your dreams are the strong limiting beliefs that you hold. Furthermore, the most critical of all your beliefs will have to do with the limiting beliefs you have about yourself.

No one can ever go beyond the self-image or self-concept he or she holds. It's impossible—beliefs determine your experience. If you can't see yourself doing it or being it, forget it. It won't happen. On the other hand, if you can hold on to the dream and clear out all the limiting beliefs that say you can't, it's yours!

With all the self-help information available today, why isn't everyone happy, and why don't people always get what they want? Why are so many people struggling to achieve something only to give up in frustration? How many self-help or motivational workshops have you attended only to have the excitement wear off after a short period of time?

What do you think is really believed by a man who affirms fifty times a day, "I'm rich. I'm rich. I'm rich"? You guessed it, he really believes that he is not rich.

He is also strengthening the thoughtform that is already keeping him from being rich. He'll soon see no results for his efforts and give up in frustration. His limiting belief could have to do with money, but most often it is a personal belief, such as the belief that he does not deserve money, or a related belief.

One of the lessons I had to learn the hard way when I began exploring belief systems was that experiences are determined by the sum total of your beliefs and your point of mental focus, your attention—not just the experience you selectively choose to create. I decided that since I had all this profound knowledge of how the universe works, I would get up the next morning and simply create what I wanted. Well, it didn't work, and as you might guess, I generated a lot of frustration and anger for myself. I guess I had a transparent belief about how I learn things—the hard way.

As we've seen, beliefs can be empowering or limiting. Limiting beliefs negate or subtract from empowering beliefs and desires. What do you get when you add +2 and –2? You're right—zero! This is the part that didn't sink in for me. I was still trapped into believing that if I tried hard enough to believe in what I wanted, I didn't have to pay attention to my limitations. And I didn't think that I had many limitations.

But there I was, using my old belief: "If I would just try harder, I could succeed." I soon learned that old beliefs continue to gain strength and become dominating. After I realized what was happening, I refocused my efforts to working on my liabilities—my limiting beliefs. Yes, I did find some—many, in fact. After a while, it became a treat to find them. It meant that I was one step closer to being clear.

To use an analogy, refer to the balance sheet illustration. Here, as in traditional accounting, are two columns: the assets (empowering beliefs) on the left and the liabilities (limiting beliefs) on the right. Each side is tallied to obtain the "total assets" on the left and the "total liabilities" on the right.

Balance Sheet	9/28	bid	

	Assets	Liabilities
1	Empowering	Limiting
2		
3	"I am rich"	"I NEVER GET
4	"I am rich"	
5	"I am rich"	WHAT I WANT!"
6	"I am rich"	
7		
8		
9		
10		
11		
12		
13		
14		
15		
16		
17		
18		
19		
20	Total Assets	Total Liabilities

At first glance, we can see that the old limiting belief "I never get what I want" is very strong and powerful from years of having energy added to it. It would take forever to add enough "I am rich" beliefs to the left side of the balance sheet and overcome the strong limiting belief. First of all, the "I am rich," in this case, is not really a belief; it's only a statement. It's a wish or, at best, a hope. If it were a belief, it wouldn't have to be continually repeated. Furthermore, every time it is repeated, the real belief, "I never get what I want," increases in strength to fulfill its original intent—to make sure that you don't.

There are basically two limiting beliefs in action here:

"I never get what I want."

"I am not rich" (implied).

For any real improvement in this situation, the belief "I never get what I want" must be eliminated.

There are numerous self-development books, tapes, and workshops available—all with good intent and of real benefit. In many cases, however, the benefit is temporary, and for a good reason. Many techniques don't address the cause of your experiences. They try to implement new techniques that focus on overpowering or going around the old situation to create a new desired state. This approach requires ongoing diligence and constant effort, which soon get tiresome and boring. The student usually gives up in frustration.

The main reason for limited success gets back to what we have been discussing—limiting beliefs. Old limiting beliefs must be removed. Trying to overpower them is not the best use of time and energy. What's required for permanent change in your experience is a shift from a focus on trying to overpower old beliefs with new ones to a focus on identifying and simply dissolving the old beliefs that no longer serve you. These limiting beliefs may have been appropriate when you were a child, but they hinder you as an adult.

It's like planting a flower garden. If you don't till the soil and pull out all the weeds before you plant, you'll end up with a field of weeds that has some flowers in it. An improvement, but not the desired result. Till the soil, remove the weeds, and then plant your seeds. In no time at all, you'll have a marvelous garden of your favorite flowers.

Another way to look at the same concept is to imagine trying to hit the bull's-eye on a target on the other side of a cornfield. The corn stalks (limiting beliefs) resist and deflect the path of the arrow. Rather than try to force the arrow through the corn by pulling harder on the string, simply remove the corn stalks between you and the target.

Now, with an accurate aim and normal pull, a bull's-eye is assured.

People spend significant effort and money looking for ways to get what they want—happiness, money, love, jobs—only to give up in frustration. The secret is to focus on dissolving barriers—the limiting beliefs that are generating your life's frustrations and fears.

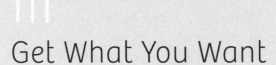

Get What You Want

Maintain a Positive Environment

Let's take the knowledge that you have gained and make it work for you. The first thing to remember is that you will experience, for some period of time, the results of the thoughtforms that you put into motion in the past. Recognize that this will occur, and begin to work from this moment forth to deliberately design the experiences you wish to have in the future.

What you need to do is create a positive environment for yourself while you explore prior choices that will continue to impact you. Begin creating a positive attitude about life by establishing your own version of "Everything works for me easily and effortlessly." I say "your version" because that's what is important. It's your beliefs that count—not mine.

It will take a little practice, but as you strengthen your empowering thoughtform, you'll notice a difference in your emotional response. Adopt the philosophy that you can learn something from every experience.

To further enhance your environment, focus on the positive things around you. See the glass as half full rather than half empty. Be sure to focus your attention on what you want, not on what you don't want. If you desire more money, focus on how to obtain more—not on the fact that you don't have enough. Constantly keep in mind what you've learned about thoughtforms: you don't want to use your energy to strengthen limiting ones. Keep your attention focused on your desires and goals; strengthen those thoughtforms. Your overall intent should be to keep your energy positive. And you know what that means—the more you stay positive, the more you will attract positive experiences.

There are times, however, when you won't feel positive. That's only being human. I'm not encouraging you to deny or avoid unpleasant feelings or situations. Experiencing them is an important part of your growth process. I'm saying to experience them, but move on as quickly as possible. Develop your ability to emotionally rebound. As you remove limiting beliefs, doing so will become easier and easier.

I have a friend who was told by a counselor that to release his fears he needed to experience them. That may be true, but the experience need not last for years. Experience and release can be done in a matter of minutes.

I used to have fun with my management team when something went wrong and we all felt discouraged. I'd say, "OK, we are going to sit here for five minutes and suck our thumbs and then forget it." We did and it worked. How long can you feel depressed when you're looking at five other grown men sucking their thumbs?

Have Faith in Yourself

It's important also that you have the faith (belief) that you can make the changes in your life that you choose to make. If you have the belief that you can't help yourself change, stop right where you are, because your disbelief will negate anything that you attempt to do. Remember, you can change only what you are willing to accept responsibility for. So create your version of "I'm responsible for my own experiences, and I can change my life for the better." You can do it! Just believe it. Believe in yourself.

I would encourage you not to establish expectations that everything in your life will miraculously change overnight. If it does, that's wonderful. Based on my experience, however, it may take some patience on your part. That may sound like a limiting statement, but I'd rather see you make incremental progress and stick with it than go for the moon and quit in frustration. Your library of beliefs was built up over a number of years; it will take some research to access the inventory. The time to start the process of change, however, is right now.

Process is an important word. A process is something that happens over time. Change is a process. Unfortunately, most of us want change to be an event, with instantaneous results. Life itself is a process—ever changing, ever unfolding.

You're probably wondering how long your process of change will take. Realistically? Forever! Don't panic—you'll want to continue your own process of growth and change to expand and deepen your experiences indefinitely. It becomes compelling. Personal growth is a lifelong process. So change what you want to change—at your own pace. You are experiencing your world. You call the shots.

Increase Your Self-Awareness

With the appropriate emotional environment established and the confidence that you can succeed, now you need to expand your awareness of yourself so you can begin to recognize your limiting beliefs.

Phrase Completion

One of the easiest ways of bringing your beliefs to the surface is to do simple phrase-completion exercises. The concept involves spontaneously completing the endings to certain phrases to allow the subconscious mind to bring forth uncensored information. When you get your logical, rational thought processes involved, you begin judging the information, and the free flow ceases. The Beliefs Mapping Exercise in section IV will help you surface some of your limiting beliefs. To get a better feel for the concept, take a look at a few examples in the illustration.

```
I am married.
I am tall.
I am fat.
I am worried a worrier.
I am old.
I am always late.
I am kind.
I am poor.
I am never satisfied.
I am . . .
```

Notice the number of limiting beliefs that surfaced in this phrase-completion list. Do any of them look familiar?

Monitor Your Self-Talk

Monitoring your self-talk is an excellent way to start collecting data on what beliefs you hold. Self-talk is the constant mental and/or verbal conversation that goes on as you are going about your day. It's talking to yourself. For me, it's usually mental. I am happy to say that since I started removing my limiting thoughtforms, much of my critical self-talk has vanished. I can now find time to just experience the moment. You can do the same.

What usually happens when you're involved in self-talk is that you are not present mentally to experience the *now* that we discussed earlier. Self-talk has you either chewing over something that has already happened or agonizing over something that you're afraid will happen. Most of this self-talk is very limiting; it's often about something you did or didn't do or about what someone else did or didn't do. Generally, it is nonproductive and judgmental. On the other hand, if you spend your day telling yourself how wonderful you are, that's great.

You can learn a lot about your limiting beliefs by being an observer of your self-talk. Make believe you are a miniature private investigator, and sit on your shoulder and take notes. What's this person focused on? Listen to your own beliefs. Write them down. How many of them are self-critical? Self-criticism is very limiting. Learn to enjoy catching yourself in the act. "Aha, gotcha again."

Another approach to self-talk would be to ask a committed listener, such as your spouse, a significant other, or a trusted friend, to assist you by writing down what they hear you say, especially when you are upset. Just be sure you are ready for it—no denial, no being defensive, and please don't shoot the messenger! Just note the beliefs that they recorded and decide what you want to do with them. Are some of them limiting you?

Notice Your Reflections

Another technique to increase your awareness is to monitor your reflections in the universal mirror. Recall from the discussion on mirroring that the events, circumstances, and people that show up in your life are there to mirror back to you what you're projecting into the universe. To illustrate what I mean by events reflecting back to you, I'll share a personal experience with you.

One of my idiosyncrasies is orderliness. Everything must be in its place, and things must be kept clean and tidy at all times. Normally this trait is an asset, but taken to extremes, it becomes a liability. One of the things that irritates me is loose hair—cat hair, dog hair, human hair, it doesn't matter. For years, I've had very little hair; fortunately, my former mate liked bald heads. Her hair was beautiful—chestnut brown and very long.

One day, I was in the bathroom getting very irritated about the long brown hair that I noticed littering the floor. My mental conversation was very judgmental about my mate not cleaning up after herself. As I sat there getting more irritated, I had a jolting thought: "Oh, my god, what if there were no hair at all?"

In that moment, something shifted, and the hair on the floor became a reminder to me of how lucky I was that she was in my life. It brought tears of joy to my eyes. Does your spouse leave the top off of the toothpaste, or put the toilet paper on the roll backwards? Great! Now you have a reminder, too, of how lucky you are.

If you have not already started a list of reflections that bother you, please start one and continue to update it as situations arise. As you encounter situations that hook you, ask yourself, "What do I believe is happening here?" Make a note of your answer. At the end of the General Beliefs Mapping

Exercise on page 134, I'll give you some hints on how to process this information.

Keep in mind also what I said about reflections from other people. A judgment that you assign to someone else is a judgment you are projecting. You are essentially assigning the judgment to yourself. For example, if you notice someone else's behavior and label that person a know-it-all, what does that say about you? My guess is that it reflects your insecurity about not knowing it all.

When you judge, there is an aspect of your personality that you haven't accepted. It's probably related to not feeling smart enough or maybe feeling inadequate about not having a degree or some acceptable (to you) level of credentials or training. If you felt good about yourself, another person's behavior wouldn't hook you.

That's the mirror; it reflects back to you information that allows you to learn more about yourself. When you notice that you are judging someone, ask yourself, "If this is what I believe about that person, what does that say about me?' Remember what I said earlier about not judging yourself for judging others. It will take some time to shift your judgments—if you choose to do so. In the meantime, acknowledge yourself for having the guts to work on it.

Remove Limiting Thoughtforms

To remove limiting thoughtforms, you utilize the same method that you used when you acquired them. You used choice. To remove them, you also use choice. You just choose to do so.

This may sound too simple, but that's how it works. There are several copyrighted techniques that detail processes for removing unwanted thoughtforms, but the basic element of removal is the aspect of choice.

The actual removal step is simple, but the challenge for most people is getting to that point mentally. Can you imagine fire walking by yourself if you read in a book that all you had to do was concentrate on the belief that you are walking on wet, moist, velvety grass? I don't think you would take off your shoes until you'd had some coaching. The techniques for removing thoughtforms are of the same nature. Confidence must be built with smaller experiences of success before most people will believe that they can do it. We all have existing beliefs about what can and cannot be done. They must be dealt with first. Also, when you remove a limiting thought-form, it's a good idea to replace it with an empowering one. Here's a simple example.

Let's say that you uncovered the limiting belief "Nothing ever works for me." First, put your full concentration on that belief and then say to yourself slowly and deliberately, either mentally or verbally, "I have the belief 'Nothing works for me,' and I choose to remove it from my belief system because it limits me." (You might want to create a visualization of the belief energy disappearing or dissolving as you verbalize the release.) That's all it takes. To replace it, just choose a new one. "I choose to replace it with 'everything that I do works out for my best interest.'"

If you will recall the grape-cluster structure of thought-forms, you will notice that each time you remove a thought-form, you're working your way down the stem until you come to the root-cause thoughtform. Another way to look at it would be to convert the branches of each stem into a list, with the root thoughtform at the bottom of the list. The similar thoughtforms generated subsequently get layered on top of the previously created one. The most recently generated one would, therefore, be at the top of the list (the tip of the branch).

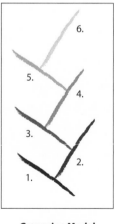

Grapevine Model

6. I can't get around like I used to.

5. I just can't make him happy.

4. My boss never liked me.

3. I'll never get into college.

2. I can't read the blackboard.

1. Something's wrong with me.

List Model

Thoughtform structure

For those with the confidence to forge ahead at removing limiting thoughtforms, here is the secret that I finally learned. Use the removing-limiting-thoughtforms technique on your doubts as well. Doubt is what used to stop me. "Did it work? Am I doing it right? It doesn't seem to be working today. Something's wrong. I need more experience! I need help." Every thought of this nature will hinder your progress because, as you've learned, thoughtforms will act to fulfill themselves. When you think, "Something's wrong," guess what you've just created. So when a doubt shows up, just use the technique to get rid of it and keep going.

Here's Another Example

Let's say you want to remove the limiting belief "Nobody cares about what I have to say." As you begin, you have the thought, "I'm not sure I know how to do this right." That now becomes the limiting belief that you work on. Start with "I have the belief 'I am not sure I know how to do this right,' and I choose to remove it from my belief system because it limits me."

Then you have the thought, "I'm not sure that worked." Do the same thing: "I have the belief 'I'm not sure that worked,' and I choose to remove it from my belief system because it limits me."

Then go to the original limiting belief, "Nobody cares about what I have to say." If another doubt shows up before you removed the original limiting belief, treat it the same way—remove it. Initially, don't be surprised if a number of these pesky doubts show up. Just cheer for yourself that you found another one and remove it. Keep going. It will get easier and easier.

IV
Thought and Belief
in Action

Section IV provides examples of the concepts related to thought and belief, and advice for using these concepts to improve different areas of your life.

In some cases, I have repeated the example for discovering your limiting beliefs because I want you to become so familiar with it that it becomes second nature to you. You may, after some practice, find yourself running the exercise mentally as you drive down the street.

If you follow this advice diligently, you will see substantial improvement in your relationships, your health, your career, your financial abundance, and your ability to manifest your desires, as well as a well-deserved sense of inner peace. You will be on your way to creating the life that *you* want.

Upgrading Your Life

If you are current with today's advertising, you are well aware that you can get an upgrade for many of the things that you now own. You can upgrade your automobile's ignition system to improve its efficiency. You can upgrade your PC to increase its computing power and memory capacity. You can upgrade your computer peripherals to wireless. You can upgrade your insurance policies and financial investments. And, if you are into remodeling, you can upgrade just about every system in your house. Upgrading is a way of life for just about everyone. It gives us the ability to keep up with life in an economical, modular fashion as our needs change.

There is another opportunity for an upgrade in your life that significantly outweighs the benefits of any other upgrade that you could ever consider. Unfortunately, not many of us are aware of the basic principle that determines our lives, so we don't give much thought to upgrading it.

The Foundation

The foundation for everything that we experience in life is derived from the thoughts that we issue into the universe and the accompanying beliefs that we hold. Our beliefs are those thoughts that we have accepted as being true for us.

They originate from our own thoughts or are accepted from others. The accumulation of all of our beliefs makes up our individual belief system—the blueprint from which we experience our life.

Most of us structured the foundation of our individual belief system years ago, when we were young. We developed beliefs about many things: our worth, our abilities, our environment, our relationship with others, our friends, our parents, money, men, women, sex, what we can and cannot do, what's right, what's wrong, just to name a few. How many of us are living our lives today with a belief system dominated by limiting beliefs that we originated in childhood? Unfortunately, most of us. If we don't upgrade our belief system to replace these limiting beliefs, we will experience much of our life from the perspective of a small child. Sound absurd? Ask yourself the following questions: Who do you need permission from to do what you want to do in life? Do you worry about hurting other people's feelings? Do you tell lies to keep from upsetting someone else? Do you behave in certain ways so someone you care about won't be upset with you? Do you spend a lot of energy on meeting other's expectations of you? Do you worry about looking good? Do you feel safe in the world? Do you worry about being a burden to others? Do you speak your mind at all times, or do you withhold your thoughts?

If you answered yes to any of these questions, you might want to consider doing some upgrading. Every one of these questions points to something in your belief system that keeps you from being emotionally free—free to be truly be yourself.

The Upgrade

"So," you ask, "now that I am aware that I could benefit from an upgrade, how do I go about it? What do I have to do to uncover and upgrade my limiting beliefs?"

Begin by using the universe as a mirror. Treat every experience you encounter as a reflection of your belief system. Pay close attention to experiences that are highly charged with emotion. You are not looking for something wrong; you're just noticing what's there—becoming more aware. If something shows up that you don't like, just ask yourself, "What would I have to believe to be having this experience?" Continue asking and answering—repeatedly—"What other belief would I have to hold to be having this experience?" until you reach an answer that feels like an "aha." When you have a sudden realization—it will probably have emotion associated with it—you've reached the deep-seated root-cause belief that is generating your undesirable experience. With this new awareness, you can now begin upgrading your belief system with more empowering beliefs.

To gain optimum benefit from this technique, look at the major areas of your life, such as self-esteem, relationships, money, sex, and career, for undesirable circumstances and see if you can root out and upgrade the limiting beliefs.

An upgrade of your belief system will provide you with the emotional freedom that you deserve. As you upgrade, you will notice that your life becomes calmer and more free flowing. Your desires will seem to manifest effortlessly. Go for it! Upgrading your belief system will be your best investment ever—guaranteed!

Living in Appreciation

When I was a small boy, I spent a lot of time with my grandparents. Before each meal, Pop-Pop would say grace: "Dear Jesus, as our heads we bow, we thank thee for this food. Amen." Pop-Pop's words didn't mean much to me then. They were just something we were supposed to say before meals. But looking back, I see that his prayer is one of my first recollections of appreciation. He was expressing his appreciation for our food.

When I went to bed, my mother would always insist that I say my prayers: "Now I lay me down to sleep. I pray the Lord my soul to keep. If I should die before I wake, I pray the Lord my soul to take." Another expression of appreciation—this one for my life.

As we grow up, we are taught the appropriate ways of expressing appreciation. We learn to say thank you, clap our hands, bow, give gifts, smile, and shout out loud. Our expressions of appreciation usually are extended to another person or a seemingly higher power as a means of showing our gratitude for something we received.

Another aspect of appreciation is to hold something or someone in awe—holding it, him, or her in high esteem. We might appreciate something because it's a powerful symbol, like the American flag, or because it's emotionally moving, like something of rare beauty. We might also appreciate an experience that touches us deeply, like gazing at the stars and contemplating the vastness of the universe. Appreciating is something most of us do—on occasion.

Can you imagine being in a state of appreciation all the time? When you are appreciating something or someone, how do you feel? You feel good, don't you? That's the first clue—feelings. Isn't that what we are all striving for—to feel good?

We usually say we want to be successful, but what that really means for most of us is to experience feeling good. When we feel good, there isn't much more that we desire. Our energy is positive and light, and we attract more positive situations, circumstances, and events into our life. Life seems to flow effortlessly.

So it would seem that all we have to do to feel good all the time is to stay in appreciation. But I'm sure you already are conjuring up a list of all the things or people you know that you could not appreciate no matter how hard you tried.

When you find something or someone that you can't appreciate, what is it that keeps you from appreciating it? It's a judgment you have, isn't it? That's the secret: to stay in appreciation, you have to give up judgment.

Since the printing of James Redfield's *Celestine Prophecy* and Deepak Chopra's *Seven Spiritual Laws of Success*, the subject of being nonjudgmental has become quite popular. At a recent workshop, with eighty persons in attendance, the audience was asked, "How many of you are working on being nonjudgmental?" Nearly everyone raised their hands. After some discussion, it became clear that giving up judgment was quite challenging. Now that people were more aware of being judgmental, they were now being critical (judgmental) of themselves for having judgmental thoughts, further compounding the problem.

Being nonjudgmental doesn't mean to stop talking about the person or item you have critical thoughts about. It means eliminating the critical thoughts altogether. To my knowledge, there is only one way to do it, and that is to eliminate the source of the critical thoughts. And that is done by removing the limiting beliefs that are creating the critical thoughts, and learning to focus your attention on the present moment, not on the past or the future.

Focusing on the present moment helps keep you out of worry, fear, and doubt while you work on removing the limiting beliefs that are generating your worry, fear, and doubt. Focusing on the present moment helps you focus on and appreciate what you have, not what you don't have. By focusing on what you have, you can stay in appreciation. You can be grateful for what you have even if there are things that you may want to change in the future. If you focus on the fact that you don't have something, you fall out of being in appreciation, your energy becomes negative, you feel lousy, and you attract more of the state of being in lack.

Remember, your creative energy follows your attention. And what you focus your attention on expands in your life. So begin by appreciating, in each moment, what you have, and you will attract more of it. You will begin creating whatever you need, moment by moment.

Stop for a moment and ask your self honestly, "Do I have everything that I need in this moment?" Not what you may ultimately want, but what you need. If you have everything you need in this moment, can't you appreciate and be thankful for what you have? If you extrapolate that experience to each future moment, you always will have everything you need.

With your attention focused in the moment, start looking for the limiting beliefs that are generating your critical thoughts. Ask yourself, "What would I have to believe to experience these thoughts (name the ones that bother you the most)?" Continue asking yourself—repeatedly—"What other belief could I hold to be experiencing these thoughts?" until you uncover the root belief generating the judgmental thoughts. You will have a sudden realization—and maybe a few tears—when you uncover it. The belief was most likely related to some painful situation about which you made a decision (created a belief). Now, from a new perspective, you can choose to change it.

As you work your way though your library of beliefs with this simple technique—removing the limiting ones— you will notice that your judgmental thoughts diminish, and your mind becomes more peaceful. It may take a while, so be patient with yourself. If you continue to work on removing your limiting beliefs and stay focused in the moment on what you have, you will be on your way to living in appreciation. Can one live in appreciation all the time? It's worth a try. Go for it!

Experiencing Your Choices

When I was young and things got difficult at home—usually between my mother and me—I would run off to my grandmother's house. It wasn't much of an investment in courage because it was only two blocks away. It did, however, provide me with immediate refuge from whatever situation I was escaping. Mom-Mom, as I called my grandmother, was careful never to take sides and always had chocolate-chip cookies in the owl-shaped cookie jar on the kitchen stove. She also let me sit in her cozy lap while we listened to the radio.

Mom-Mom always had lots of food in the house, and it was readily available. She always said, "You can take as much as you want, but you must eat everything you take." She didn't like wasting anything, especially food. That rule seemed fine with me and helped me remain guilt free as I topped off my pockets with cookies and candy every time I left the kitchen.

One evening at dinner, I put much more food on my plate than I could eat. As Mom-Mom put it, "Your eyes were bigger than your belly." Even with my pleading, she would not back down. She made me sit there until my plate was clean. It took several hours, and I was very ill. It was an experience I will never forget. That was the last time I made a pig of myself at Mom-Mom's house.

Little did I realize that that incident was a prime example of how we live our lives. It was about making choices we have to live with.

The real choices we make in life are the thoughts that we think and the beliefs that we hold as truth. Our thoughts and beliefs exist as minute waves of energy that operate in the universe to create the situations, circumstances, and relationships we experience as our life. And the universe is just like Mom-Mom—it gives you no slack. If you put thought energy into the universe, you must experience it. "As ye sow, so shall ye reap," says the Bible. And, as you know, at times, it can be very uncomfortable experiencing your own creations.

The good news is that once you recognize that you are the source of your own experiences, you gain control over your life. Being the source, or cause, means that you can change situations that are giving you difficulty rather than blaming someone else or some other power.

It's a very simple concept once you understand it. But it is startling news for many, because it clearly says that we are all responsible for our own life situations. At first, many of us are not ready for such responsibility. When I was first introduced to the concept that "beliefs determine experience," I certainly didn't believe that I was responsible for all the seeming disasters that happened in my life. But there is nothing like good old experience to get one knowing the truth.

Most of us can see the results of the conscious choices that we make in our lives and, with a little contemplation, can recognize the link between our choices and the resulting experience. What's unknown to most of us is that every moment of our lives, we are also making choices from beliefs that we are not consciously aware of. These subconscious beliefs, in many cases, adversely impact what we are consciously choosing.

Here, as a reminder, is the simple technique that will help you shed some light on the subconscious beliefs that might be getting in your way. Ask yourself, "What would I have to believe to have that experience?" Continue asking and answering this question for yourself until you reach an answer that feels like an "aha." When you have a sudden realization—it will probably have emotion associated with it—you've reached the deep-seated, root-cause belief that is generating your undesirable experience. As you take responsibility for both your subconscious and conscious choices, you'll feel more confident and motivated to ferret out your limiting beliefs.

You deserve to experience all of your desires. Continue removing those restrictive limits, and let your power shine through.

Say Good-Bye to Rejection

At some point in our lives we all come face to face with feelings of rejection. These feelings can be brought about by many situations. A lover, partner, spouse, or a close friend decides that they want out of the relationship; a parent declines an offer to visit for the holidays; the company you desperately want to work for turns down your application; your family doesn't like what you just spent hours cooking. Think of the last time you felt rejected. What were the circumstances?

For most of us, the feelings related to being rejected are so severe that we will do most anything to avoid putting ourselves in a situation where they may be triggered. Selling products is a big trigger for a lot of people because they fear the feelings that would arise should someone say no to them. Sales trainers often condition new sales-persons by having them assume they are going to hear no fifty times. The trainers create excitement about each no by telling salespeople it is getting them closer to the first yes. This may work on the surface, but the underlying fear is still there. "But what if I hear no 100 times?" someone might think.

Let's examine the circumstances related to feeling rejected. First, where do our feelings originate? What causes them? You guessed it: our feelings come from our own thoughts. That means that our feelings are self-determined and not caused by someone else. No one else can generate our thoughts. They are ours and, consequently, so are our feelings. The thoughts about being rejected come from our own perception of what happened. That means that the event—the rejection—doesn't exist. It's only our mental perception of the event that labels it *rejection*.

Reframing Rejection

Several years ago when I was doing career counseling, some of my clients would refer to the rejection letters they received in response to mailing their resume. As they described the circumstances in detail, I could see that they felt personally rejected. They were taking the rejection letter to heart. Their perception of having been rejected was having a very negative impact on their attitude—not a good situation for conducting a job search.

To help them shift their perspective so they could keep their energy positive, I created a simple exercise. See if it works for you.

Imagine several small items on a tabletop. One is made of rubber, one of wood, one of glass, one of plastic, and one of iron. Now visualize a magnet about the same size as the other objects. Imagine moving the magnet to the rubber, then to the wood, and in turn to the glass and the plastic. What happened? Nothing. Now move the magnet to the iron. What happened? Smack! The magnet and iron stuck together. Why? Because their properties attract each other. They are a good match.

Did the rubber, the wood, the glass, and the plastic reject the magnet? Of course not. They just had different characteristics. They were just not the right match. No rejection at all. The magnet only needed to find the right match for it.

So when you find yourself in a situation that could be labeled rejection, think of it instead as just a situation that doesn't match you. Simply say to yourself, "There is a better fit for me." Then go on, anticipating that you will find a situation that is a perfect match for you.

The situation is slightly different when you confront a verbal no, but it's still your perception that labels the response a rejection. When someone says no, they are merely stating their preference. Their preference says nothing about you. So when someone says no to you, remind yourself that they are merely expressing a preference. Sometimes it helps to say to yourself, "This is not about me." These simple techniques are useful for shifting your feelings once they are triggered.

Eliminate Rejection by Releasing Limiting Beliefs

To truly eliminate rejection from your life, you need to eliminate what's *really* triggering your feelings: a belief that you are most likely not aware of. At some prior time in your life you encountered a situation that was painful, and you made a decision (created a belief) about what happened. Because the situation was painful, you unknowingly tucked it away in what is referred to as your subconscious. Now, when similar situations occur, those same painful feelings you felt during the original situation arise automatically. You seem to have no control over them.

Our perceptions and experiences are derived from our beliefs. Recall the simple exercise that can help you find out what belief is creating your feelings of rejection.

Identify a situation that triggers your feelings of rejection. Call your feelings of rejection "that feeling." Then ask yourself, "What would I have to believe to experience that feeling?" Continue asking and answering—repeatedly— "What other belief might I hold to experience that feeling?" until you reach an answer that feels like an "aha." When you have a sudden realization—it will probably have emotion associated with it—you've reached the deep-seated, root-cause belief that is generating your feelings of rejection. With this new awareness, you can now replace that limiting belief with an empowering one.

Don't be surprised if you uncover a belief that you have about yourself. When we don't feel good about ourselves, we look to others to validate our worth. When we don't get it, we feel rejected. When we value ourselves, rejection isn't usually an issue.

If you encounter feelings of rejection, explore your beliefs and release those that are limiting you. It's the path for saying good-bye to those feelings—*forever.*

Put the Love Back in Your Relationship

When Sidney and Jane fell in love, they were so close that it would have been almost impossible to slide a piece of greased wax paper between them. They were inseparable. The love they felt overrode anything that could possibly occur to disrupt their constant state of bliss.

It wasn't long before Sidney did something that Jane didn't like. She let him know, in no uncertain terms, that he was to never do it again. Sidney grudgingly complied; he would never do it again. But what he did was create a "withhold" for himself. In the future, Sidney would withhold his action, not because he wanted to, but because he was accommodating Jane. Sidney's creation of a withhold put a portion of their relationship off limits. With the creation of the withhold, a landmine, so to speak, was placed in the space between them. "Don't step there—you'll create an explosion." Repeatedly withholding is commonly called "collecting stamps." In addition, Sidney was suppressing his self-expression; he was denying himself. Self-denial creates resentment.

Within days, Jane said something that Sidney didn't like, and he unloaded on her. "Whoops, better not bring that subject up again," Jane decided, creating another withhold. Another landmine was placed in the space between them. Gradually, more and more of their relationship was classified as off limits. It didn't take long, with this game of withhold ping-pong, before the space between Sidney and Jane was nearly filled to capacity with landmines set to explode with the slightest misstep. The tension and resentment between them escalated with each new mine.

A few years later, Sidney and Jane sat across from each other at the dinner table, and there was nothing safe to talk about. Almost everything in their relationship was off limits.

Sound familiar? What happened?

First of all, when someone in a relationship is upset, his or her upset is never about what is occurring at the moment. It's about something that occurred in the past and that is being triggered again by the other person's actions or words. So if Sidney's original action triggered Jane's anger, her upset isn't his responsibility. *The person with the emotion is responsible for the emotion.* Therefore, there is no need for Sidney to consider defending himself. And it's not to Jane's benefit for him to withhold his action in the future. By withholding, he is taking away the trigger that Jane needs to help her resolve the issue. She needs to resolve what's *underneath* her anger, so her upset won't happen again. If Jane were emotionally free, Sidney could do what he did, and while Jane might notice it and comment on it, she'd have no emotional reaction. It's the emotional reaction that let's you know that there is a healing opportunity at hand.

I'm not suggesting that you deliberately go around pushing your partner's buttons. What I am suggesting is that you be yourself. If your action accidentally triggers your partner, remember that your partner's reaction is not your responsibility. Your partner's emotions are generated by his/her thoughts, and his/her thoughts develop from his/her belief system. *The source of the emotion is the person with the emotion.* (If this idea were understood by more of us, there would be a lot less interpersonal conflict.)

During an upset, your partner's emotions are most likely the result of an unconscious belief—a limiting belief that your partner isn't aware of—being activated by the incident. With the following simple routine, you can help him or her bring the limiting belief into conscious awareness for release.

When your partner gets upset, stay energetically connected (don't withdraw), refrain from getting hooked yourself, and provide a loving space for your partner to explore what he or she believes is happening. You might gently say, "What do you believe just happened?" When you get an answer, no matter how illogical it is, gently ask, "When was the last time you felt this way?" Take that answer and, after each answer, keep repeating the question "And before that?" until your partner uncovers the original incident that resembles what just occurred. Your partner will have a sudden "aha" realization and receive insight about the limiting belief that created the upset. This realization will usually release the belief, along with the emotional energy it generated. You might need to provide a box of tissues and a few hugs. The original incident was most likely painful.

Each time you and your partner handle one of these situations, you explode the associated landmine, and the healing that takes place fills the hole with love. So if you want to put the love back in your relationship, you must both agree to always be yourself. And if a landmine does go off, you will support each other in the healing process—no more withholds. Blow up the mines, and fill the holes with love. It takes diligence, but it will put the love back—guaranteed.

The Mission

Dear Citizen:

Your personal characteristics and experience have been brought to the attention of the selection committee for a top-secret mission. The only thing I can tell you at this time is that the mission involves the development of a new species that will inhabit a yet-to-be-chosen—and still-to-be-discovered—planet outside of our solar system.

The experiment that you will participate in, if you are chosen, has great rewards for you personally, but you must also know that it involves great risk. Only you can determine the outcome of your particular mission.

Your analytical ability will be vitally important, because the makeup of the planet's basic life elements will have to be determined to ensure your physical safety. Your degree of emotional sensitivity will be critical, because experience on the new planet will be based on "feelings." You will certainly encounter other cultures on your adventure, and you will be required to effectively communicate your sincere intentions at all times. The honesty reflected in your eyes—the windows to the soul—and your leadership presence will support you well. Your intellect will be fully challenged, and you will have to use every ounce of entrepreneurial capability you can muster.

Funding for the selected candidates' return has not yet been approved; therefore, you may have to depend on your own resources. Unfortunately, until the mission is complete, you will have to forego your close ties to family support. You will truly be on your own.

The basic elements of the experiment on the new planet, though very simple in nature, will require your sharpest skills and utmost determination if you are to successfully complete the mission. The basic elements of reality for the new planet are as follows:

"Thought" will be the basis of creation on this new

planet, and the thoughts generated will be separate energy forms whose sole purpose is to carry out the intent of the thought. Consequently, the inhabitants of the new planet will experience, based on their own feelings, the reality created by their individual belief systems (i.e., the thoughts that they believe to be true, will be true—for them).

For example, if an inhabitant believes that she or he is "not deserving," that individual, no matter how hard she or he tries, will be unable to find what she or he is seeking. This principle will apply in all regards—relationships, job satisfaction, financial abundance. This way, each individual will be totally responsible for his or her own reality. They will have no one or nothing else to blame for their own life experiences.

Since the elements of reality on the new planet are so simple, you will have to, as part of your trial, undergo a complete deprogramming of the complexity of beliefs you have accepted as truth during your lifetimes in our solar system.

Your first stop on your trial journey is at the waterfall of discovery deep in the heart of the Amazoid jungle, many miles from your present civilization. At the waterfall, you will be given directions (just listen for guidance in the stillness) on how you can become aware of all the limitations you have accepted as truth during your lifetimes. Guidance will tell you how you can now release all of these limitations and discover the real you. This will not be a long process (the speed of discovery depends on your ability to spend reflective time with yourself), and if all goes well, you will emerge from the waterfall experience with a true picture of who you really are. You will have admiration and love for yourself and the unique person that you are. You will no longer feel the need to live your life for others; instead, you will recognize it is your life to experience and enjoy to the fullest extent.

Upon leaving the waterfall and all of its majesty, you will follow a clearly marked path that extends many, many miles through dense and treacherous terrain. Your final task, to determine the effectiveness of your work at the waterfall, will be for you to find your way back to your own sector of our civilization.

The path will contain many forks, where you will have to determine, based on the conditions at hand, which choice is the best choice for you—the choice that you prefer. The correct choices at each fork will bring you safely back home, where you will not only experience a life with inner peace and fulfillment, but you will also have qualified for participation in the experiment on the new planet—that is, if you still choose to do so.

If you make any choices that are based on not loving yourself, we regret to tell you that the path chosen has no end. It merely wanders aimlessly through the jungle, providing you with a life of discontent and unfulfilled expectations. Please choose carefully; our civilization doesn't want to lose people with your potential. And the experimental mission to the new planet desperately needs your talents.

Oh, by the way, I have just been informed that I am now free to tell you the name of the new planet. It will be called Earth.

Have a safe journey,
The Commander

Take Back Your Power

If you are up on your astrology, you are aware that relationships that are not whole have been dealt a tremendous blow. Astrological forces are forcing either the resolution of imbalances or total destruction. Destruction enables a total rebirth or provides an opening for the birth of a new relationship based on a new healthier paradigm of relating.

For a relationship to be whole, both parties must be whole. By *whole,* I mean totally self-sufficient regarding their ability to love themselves and provide their own inner nurturing. Many would say being whole means having a healthy inner child.

Unhealthy relationships contain codependency, where one or both parties fill their inner void through the other person. When one person leaves the relationship, the dependent person feels emotionally destroyed. When this happens, traditional healing therapy and the person's friends say that he or she must "let go" to facilitate healing. Letting go is quite difficult for most people, because what they are being asked to let go of is the nurturing that they so desired in the first place. And trying to let go only keeps the dependent person's attention focused on the former partner he or she is trying to let go of, which deepens the pain.

A better way to regain the energetic emotional balance needed in this situation is to realize what really happened. The pain is there because the codependent party gave away their power to the other person. So instead of focusing on letting go of the other person who provided all or most of their nurturing—consciously or not—the codependent person needs to pull back his or her power.

If you find yourself in this position, try the following visualization after you have reached a state of relaxation. Visualize yourself and your partner separated by some comfortable distance. Then, like a fisherman, start reeling your power back as if you were reeling in a trophy-sized fish. Reel the regained power (your self-love) slowly into your heart. If you see your partner pulling back, continue reeling. Reel him or her right into your heart and dissolve him or her with unconditional love. Next, take the self-love that you have now regained and move it from your heart down to your inner child, where it can begin the inner healing that is needed. Your task now is to focus on *yourself* and heal your inner child by providing the love and nurturing you need for you own wholeness.

Take the pain you have been feeling, in whatever form it materializes for you, and visualize putting it in a purple bag to be carried off for transmutation back into universal energy. Fill the painful void—usually in the solar-plexus area—with a big red heart symbolizing your new regained love for yourself.

Until you feel completely healed, continue to focus on loving your inner child—your true self. With your attention off your former partner, you will have less pain and be able to heal much faster. You have regained your power in the form of self-love. With a healthy love of self, you will never want to give your power away again. What you will do in the future is give away the love that *overflows* from your love of self.

If you find that you have a difficult time with the concept of self-love, write down all the beliefs you have about yourself. What is it that keeps you from loving yourself—guilt, shame, a physical characteristic, or possibly failure? If so, it's time for some forgiveness.

We have all experienced difficult situations in the past. Let them go! You did the best you could at the time. Stop beating yourself up! Release the limiting beliefs about past situations and move on. You deserve to experience a life of emotional freedom. Love yourself, so you, in turn, can extend your love to others. Remember, you can't give away what you do not have. You will have no love to give away unless you've given love to yourself first.

Happy Thoughts

Have you ever wondered why you feel the way you do—sometimes happy, sometimes not? Remember the last time you felt really happy. What was happening? Can you recall what you were thinking at the time? That's the clue— what were you *thinking?* It's my guess that you were thinking happy thoughts. Happy thoughts make you feel happy. Sad thoughts make you feel sad. Angry thoughts make you feel angry. The way you feel depends on what you are thinking.

It's very important to understand that *your thoughts create your feelings*. What does that mean? First, it means no one else can think your thoughts; therefore, *you* are the only one who determines how you feel. You are responsible for your own happiness. Second, it means that to have happy feelings, you need to have happy thoughts.

"But," you say, "Sometimes I don't feel happy. How can I change my thoughts so I can feel happy again?"

First, when you are feeling not happy, allow yourself to feel those feelings. When you allow yourself to feel them for a few moments, they will pass. All of your feelings are a part of you, and they just want some attention. Just say to yourself, "It's OK to feel this way." When you feel your unhappy feelings, they will quickly go away. You can then get back to being happy.

Now think of something that makes you happy. Do you have a funny friend? Do you have a special place that you like to visit? Do you have a favorite food? How about a cuddly pet? Is there a song that you love to listen to or sing? What else can you think of that makes you happy?

I have a friend who has a huge teddy bear with a very comical face. It's almost impossible to look at the bear without smiling. Do you have a toy or a stuffed animal with a happy face?

Another technique to restore happy thoughts would be to repeat to yourself "I am happy" until you feel happy. It won't take long before you are smiling again.

Here's another trick to bring back that happy feeling. Find a friend and get him or her to agree to repeat after you. Say the following phrases, and wait for your friend to repeat each phrase before you go on to the next one.

You: Ha.

Your friend: Ha.

You: Ha ha.

Your friend: Ha ha.

You: Ha ha ha.

Your friend: Ha ha ha.

Keep adding *ha*'s as you go. Before long, you will both be roaring with laughter and feeling happy again.

Always think happy thoughts—and be happy.

The Secret to Achieving Emotional Freedom

Do you sometimes lose your temper or find yourself being defensive or judgmental when someone else says something? If your answer is yes, there is a simple secret to freeing yourself from those uncomfortable emotions. Knowing the secret will make a huge difference in your life—especially in your relationship with others.

When something triggers your defensiveness or judgment, some folks would say, "You got your button pushed." The secret stems from knowing what is implied by that comment.

Think of a button, like the one associated with your doorbell. The button is wired to a bell that reacts when the button is pushed, permitting electricity to flow to energize the doorbell. When the bell is energized, it reacts with sound.

The bell's reaction is an analogy to your emotional reactions (such as anger, defensiveness, judgment). In essence, you have an imaginary button connected to your emotional doorbell via your belief system. Certain external circumstances push your imaginary doorbell and energize one of your limiting beliefs. External circumstances will usually trigger a range of different beliefs that match the circumstance. The secret to experiencing emotional freedom is to uncover a limiting core belief.

A limiting core belief is usually a very strong negative generalization about people, places, or things. Based on my experience, I believe our most powerful beliefs fall into three key areas: (1) our beliefs about our self, (2) our beliefs about our relationship to others, and (3) our beliefs about the environment in which we live. And the most powerful beliefs that impact our lives are the first ones—the beliefs that we hold about our self.

Think of the people that are close to you. Look at their life circumstances, and then reflect on their beliefs and the comments that they make about the three key areas mentioned above—especially about themselves. Do you see a correlation between what they believe and what they are experiencing in their life? Do you think they are taking charge and deliberately creating their life? Or are they victims, feeling that they have no power and the world is doing everything to them?

Those who have the least emotional freedom are the victims. They blame everyone else for their life circumstances and react accordingly. They are not comfortable with who they are, and they spend a lot of energy pretending they are someone else. They usually try to act as someone else wants them to, so they can be accepted or loved. They have no emotional freedom to just be themselves. Their lack of self-worth sets the stage for having no emotional freedom. When people's self-esteem is solid, they can stand firm, without overreacting, no matter what someone else says or does. They can observe a situation without getting their button pushed or, as some would say, getting hooked.

If you get hooked or get your button pushed, here is what it's all about: you are falsely believing that when something happens "out there," *the situation says something about you,* and you react.

Typically, you're reacting to something you feel insecure about or don't like about yourself. While you work on discovering what that is, here is the secret to staying calm: when you begin to react, say quietly to yourself, "That says nothing about me." Saying this to yourself is guaranteed to immediately release the emotional charge, because you have depersonalized the situation. By depersonalizing a situation, you can remain energetically connected and emotionally detached.

With practice, you will be able to defuse many upsets before they start. You will begin to expand your ability to remain calm in any situation.

That's the secret! Now enjoy your newfound sense of peace.

How Long Will It Take Me to Find a New Job?

This was a frequently asked question by many of my former career-counseling clients who have just been laid off, usually due to a reduction in force and, in most cases, through no direct fault of their own. Job-search books and outplacement manuals usually contain information aimed at answering this question, saying the answer depended on issues such as the present state of the job market, the geographic area involved, the individual's job type and compensation level, and the amount and quality of effort invested in job hunting.

Even though these factors are recognized and understood by most job seekers, the seekers rarely, if ever, consider the most critical factor affecting the search: what the seeker believes about his or her situation and, more importantly, about him- or herself.

Power resumes, creative cover letters, and polished job-search techniques are all ineffective if candidates have less-than-positive beliefs about their new job possibilities or about their own value or self-worth.

Many of us pay some attention to positive thinking, but few realize the true power of our individual thoughts and beliefs. All of our life experiences tie directly to our own thoughts and beliefs. Our thoughts, though invisible to us, are minute packets of energy that exist (1) to fulfill the intent of the thought and (2) to attract other thoughts that are similar.

Thoughts that we have accepted as true become part of our personal belief system. Our thoughts control our emotions and, therefore, what we experience. Visualization exercises that yield experiential sensations—such as puckering up as you imagine tasting a lemon or smiling as you think of a puppy, kitten, or loved one—demonstrate how thoughts control experience.

Do you know anyone who frequently says "I hate myself," yet is healthy, happy, and prosperous? Do you know anyone who is financially prosperous, yet believes he or she is poor? Do you know anyone who is slim and trim, yet believes he or she is fat? Do you know anyone who can do something that he or she believes he or she can't?

How long do you think it will take you to get a new job if you believe your friend who says, "There are no jobs out there" or "For every $10,000 of salary, it will take you a month to find a new position"? Don't get hooked into the general beliefs that the masses subscribe to. These beliefs don't have to be true for you. What you honestly believe is what you will create and experience in your life. Believing is believing—not hoping. Hoping for something is not the same as believing. Believing contains no doubt.

When you're making a job change, for whatever reason, you're involved in a transition. For most of us, the transition involves a difficult psychological process, requiring us to leave behind an old identity to take on a new one. Transitions typically have three stages:

The End—saying good-bye with feelings of loss, grief, and sometimes anger.

The Neutral Zone—being in limbo, with feelings of confusion and no sense of direction or purpose.

The New Beginning—renewed clarity and vitality, with feelings of excitement and anticipation.

What you believe about the change has a major impact on the outcome of your job search. The unsuccessful job seeker will often get emotionally stuck, unable to let go of the past and move forward with positive enthusiasm about new career possibilities.

Limiting beliefs about being betrayed or victimized by a former employer, accompanied by feelings of bitterness, resentment, anger, and negativity, can keep a job seeker emotionally stuck for many weeks. Remaining in this emotional state will significantly inhibit the job-search process. Events, people, and circumstances will arise to support the limiting belief of being a victim. If a new job is found, it will most likely lead to the individual being victimized at work or being laid off again. Individuals who are down on themselves, feel powerless, and are still smoking about what happened to them just don't attract favorable responses, interviews, and new opportunities.

The most successful job seeker will see the layoff as a positive event—if not initially, then in a short period of time—and move on with excitement and the anticipation of new opportunities. These job seekers usually arrive at the belief that they are "lucky to be out of that place," while the unlucky ones are still employed, but waiting for the next shoe to drop.

Layoff circumstances are many and varied, but whatever they are, the past is the past. It's over. Let go and move forward with positive beliefs about your future. Potential employers will quickly sense your energy and respond accordingly. Be positive and enthusiastic; these qualities are contagious.

My experience working as a career counselor strongly supports my belief that the most important factor in how long it takes to find a new job relates to the seekers' beliefs about themselves. Those who have high self-esteem and are positive, confident, and enthusiastic about achieving a well-thought-out, focused goal are the ones who get the ideal jobs. They don't panic and take the first job that comes along. They believe that they deserve the best and will hold out until the right opportunity comes along. Doors just seem to open for those who are not willing to compromise themselves. Those who feel good about who they are attract the best situations.

There is a one-to-one correlation between what goes out and what comes back. I've seen it time and time again—once the seekers get emotionally clear and positive, what comes back changes instantly. It's interesting to see the change and hear them say, "Things are getting better out there." What they are seeing is the reflection of what changed in themselves. It's true that we attract unto ourselves that which matches how we are being.

"How long will it take me to find a new job?" It all depends—on what you believe.

Experiencing Personal Power

If you have read any of the recent books and articles about today's children, young adults, and our future leaders, I am sure you are familiar with the terms *millennial generation, Generation Y, net generation,* or *indigo children.*

Most of the generational information highlights the behavioral characteristics of the new generation and contrasts that behavior with that of previous generations.

Having a corporate background, I was very much interested in the impact the new generation was going to have on the workplace when I read its members had attributes like:

- Strong self-esteem

- An obvious sense of self

- Difficulty with discipline and/or authority

- Aversion to following orders or directions

- Impatience

- Frustration with structured systems, routines, or processes that require little creativity

- Resistance to conforming to others' desires or trends

- In general, a constant need to know why, especially when asked or told to do something

- Spiritual intelligence and/or psychic skills[1]

My first thought was, "What is going to happen when these young people begin populating the corporate world?"

---

1. Adapted from attributes originally developed by Wendy H. Chapman, M.S., of the Metagifted Resource Organization (see *www.metagifted.org*).

To answer this question, I included a global survey of high school and college students in my doctoral dissertation on leadership and organizational transformation. What I learned was very enlightening.

Numerous books and articles about today's youth highlight their unconventional behavioral characteristics. One author considers these children narcissistic; others say they can't stay focused or they have no motivation. The authors can't understand the way youth treat their bodies (tattoos and piercing) or why they consider themselves the privileged generation. What's missing is an understanding of what is causing the observed behavior.

My sense is that today's youth have a deep-seated belief about who they are and why they are here, and that belief is very different than the beliefs of previous generations. Those of us from older generations grew up believing that we had to earn the right to be cared for, respected, or loved, especially from the man upstairs. If we wanted something, we had to prove that we deserved it. It wasn't seen as our right to have it. Measuring today's youth against these old limiting beliefs isn't justified. Today's youth know they have personal power and are not limited in what they can create.

Whether it's today's youth or you or me, we all want to feel that we can maintain our personal power. And if you want to have a life filled with good relationships, you must allow others to maintain their personal power as well.

How can we allow others their personal power? *Always provide them with choice.* When they have choice, they maintain their personal power.

Allowing others to maintain their personal power has worked wonders with my team at work. It's also what parents need to help them raise the new generation of children.

Try it! It will work wonders for you and your relationships.

Who's in There?

During part of my consulting career, I served as a contract career consultant for a large global outplacement firm. An outplacement firm supplies consulting services to a company that is planning a reduction in force (RIF).

The majority of the services provide outplacement support—career-transition workshops and individual counseling—for the affected employees. Also, prior to an RIF, career consultants provide guidance to the management team to ensure that the RIF will be conducted compassionately and in accordance with legal requirements. During those days, companies were quite generous with the "transition packages" provided to members of management, offering them extended salaries, medical benefits, and as much as a year of transition services, including an office at the outplacement firm, personal counseling, and administrative support for resumes and mailings.

On the day of an RIF, I frequently found myself in a conference room, awaiting the arrival of a senior manager who had just been terminated. Upon the manager's arrival, the human resources representative would introduce the manager to me, briefly describe the services being offered the person, and then head back to HR.

As you might guess, having just been terminated, the manager sitting in front of me was in no emotional state to digest a lengthy discussion about his or her transition program. I would allow the individual to vent and then establish a mutually agreeable time to meet in a few days to begin his or her program.

Initial meetings were usually one sided; I'd listen intently to the clients venting. Because earlier in my own career I'd had the experience of being laid off, it was easy for me to relate to my clients' state of being. During this time period, I was also doing a lot of personal-growth work related to belief systems and was sensitized to what I was hearing my clients say.

The most common initial issue from the clients' point of view was, "Why me?" Personalizing the situation—taking the view "It was done to me"—created a victim mentality that seriously lengthened the time line for a client's emotional recovery. They were completely unaware that their belief system had anything to do with what they were currently experiencing.

Now that you understand the impact of one's belief system on one's experience, can you guess what might be created by each of the following statements?

- "I hated my boss and didn't like working there."

- "I always wanted to start my own business."

- "I was always thinking about retiring early, but not this early."

- "Why do bad things always happen to me?"

- "No matter how hard I work, I can't get ahead."

Believing that one is a victim negates one's sense of personal power; therefore, one feels and acts helpless. It would often take several months for me to move a client from this emotional state to one of being willing to move forward and let the past be just that—the past.

The next challenge came when I would ask a client, "What would you like to do with the rest of your life?" After receiving a deer-in-the-headlights stare, I would hear, "What do you mean *me*? What would *I* like to do? I've never thought about what I want to do. I have a wife at home and kids in college. I have to take care of them."

My answer to these statements was a cartoon of a very old, feeble man whose body was splitting open as a very powerful, good-looking young man was forcing his way out. I would lay the cartoon in front of my client and say softly as I gently pointed to his or her chest, "Who is in there trying to get out?" That simple question, in most cases, unlocked deep primordial pain and brought forth sobbing like one rarely witnesses.

Many of us live lives of tolerance without even recognizing it—until that seed inside can be ignored no longer. It finally erupts, forcing us to go exploring, so we can find out and experience who we really are.

Do you have limiting beliefs that are keeping you from expressing your heart's desire? What's keeping you from doing what you always wanted to do?

Are you living life with gusto, or are you playing it safe to avoid something?

Did you get hurt by someone and are determined to never open up again?

If any of these questions resonate with you, please read the next section, "The Inside Resume," Part I and Part II. Then, take out a notebook and complete the General Beliefs Mapping Exercise on page 134. It will change your life—guaranteed!

The Inside Resume

Part I

The post-2008 economic climate has significantly increased the number of unemployed workers who are diligently preparing, updating, or submitting their resumes, hoping that Lady Luck will soon shine on them with a new career opportunity. You may be one of them. If that's the case, pay close attention to a new concept that I am about to share with you. It's something I call the Inside Resume. Understanding your Inside Resume will help you make major advances in your job search.

The traditional resume—the paper one—is a vital link between the job seeker and the potential new employer. Many books have been written and a great number of workshops conducted on preparing an effective resume. The resume is considered to be the job seeker's marketing brochure for opening the door to an interview. The goal of a resume is to provide sufficient factual information—highlighting important skills and career accomplishments—to entice a hiring manager to want to know more about you.

Having been a job seeker, career counselor, and a hiring manager, I fully support the concept that a well-written and properly presented resume is key to securing an interview. In addition to a solid resume, job seekers also benefit from effective networking, interviewing, and negotiating. Once these skills are mastered, you should be on your way to conducting a successful job search.

But another critical element of a job search is the Inside Resume. Just as your written resume summarizes your experiences in your external world, your Inside Resume summarizes what's happening in your internal world. The Inside Resume is a summary of the beliefs that define such things as your likes and dislikes, desires and judgments, motives and values.

It's the Inside Resume that creates your energetic state—how you are being. Your state of being, then, drives what you do (or more importantly, what you don't do), and what you do (or don't do) will determine what you have (or don't have) in your life. This is an important sequence to remember: be, do, have. It's another version of "If you always do what you've always done, you'll always get what you've always gotten."

What motivates people to do what they do? What keeps them from doing what they know they need to do, yet don't do? It's what's on their Inside Resume—what they believe.

To illustrate, consider someone, Jack, who was recently laid off. Jack's Inside Resume contains the dominant belief, "I got shafted!" How might this underlying belief affect who Jack is being? Would it be safe to say that he is probably emotional—upset, angry, resentful, feeling victimized?

If Jack were being that way, what would he be doing? He would be complaining loudly about the company, criticizing his boss, and soliciting pity from his peers. Does this behavior increase Jack's productivity? Certainly not.

If Jack were doing those things, what experience would he be having? Would he have peace? Joy? Confidence? Would he be taking action to move forward? I doubt it. Jack would likely be focused on trying to figure out "Why me? Why was *I* picked? I gave that company 120 percent. George never pulled his weight. Why is he still there? Life isn't fair."

Can you see the link between being, doing, having? If Jack doesn't change the way he is *being,* it's unlikely that he will be *doing* the things that he needs to do to move toward *having* a new job.

Jack's initial response to being laid off is quite natural. His way of being is dominated by feelings of betrayal. To change the way he is being, Jack must quickly focus on releasing his strong emotions in a productive manner. He must also change the belief about his situation to see the opportunity he has to find an even better job. Focusing on appreciating all the positive things that he already has in his life will also assist him in changing how he is being.

Jeff, Jack's friend, was laid off the same day. His Inside Resume contains the belief "It didn't have anything to do with me." What state of being does Jeff's belief create? He understands the economic situation faced by the company and realizes that his boss had to make a difficult decision about which positions to eliminate. Jeff doesn't believe the decision to lay him off was personal.

His state of being generates a totally different scenario of doing. Jeff remains positive, maintains his self-confidence, and begins taking action to find a new position. This doing moves Jeff forward closer to having what he wants—a new career position.

Eventually, Jack too will come to terms with his situation and begin taking action to find a new position. Because of the way he was being, he lost valuable time getting to doing what he needs to do to begin his job search. Jack also created self-generated misery along the way.

Can you see the difference between what was on Jack's Inside Resume and what was on Jeff's? What they experience comes from what they believe about the situation they are in. They are in the same situation, yet have two totally different experiences.

With this simple example, I hope you can clearly see that your Inside Resume—your beliefs—determine how you are being. How you are being will drive what you do (or don't do), and what you do (or don't do) will determine the success that you have (or don't have).

Look at the concept in reverse. If you are not having the success that you want, ask yourself the question, "What am I not doing?" In most cases, I'll bet that you already know what you are not doing. The real question then becomes, "What's keeping me from doing what I know I should be doing?" The answer is the way you are being. As we saw in the example above, the way you are being comes from something you believe. Are there revisions that need to be made to your Inside Resume? Is there something you believe that needs to be challenged? Remember the *be*'s: *be*liefs create *be*ing.

The biggest challenge for most job seekers is keeping up the momentum and maintaining a positive frame of mind as their job search extends from days to weeks to months. The initial shot of optimism begins to wane quickly when they don't see visible results for their efforts. They become stuck—totally immobilized, no doing.

Believe it or not, this period of time can help you make revisions to your Inside Resume—revisions that are life altering. Being laid off can be a blessing. If you are currently unemployed, are you experiencing worry, fear, and doubt? Excellent! You are in the perfect place.

I know, you think I am crazy. You're thinking, "How can anyone benefit from being worried, fearful, or in doubt?"

If you are frequently finding yourself fearful, you can turn to your Inside Resume and determine what belief about your situation is creating the fear. When you find the core limiting belief creating the fear, you have the opportunity to change it. Once changed, that cause of the unwanted emotion is gone—forever. Remember what we have already concluded: beliefs create the experience you are having. So when you change your belief, you change your experience.

Several years ago, I had a former military client who was seeking a second career in the traditional business world.

After his initial counseling session, he usually had excuses for not completing his weekly assignment. He frequently cancelled his appointment—at the last minute. When he finally did come into the office, I asked him, "Do you hide under the covers in the morning?" He looked at me in amazement and said, "How did you know?" My reply was, "I've been there." In that moment, a sense of trust was established, and he openly began discussing his fear.

Here is a technique I'd like you to try the next time you are feeling an uncomfortable emotion, such as fear. Grab a tablet and on the top of the first page write down the emotional experience you are having. What you write will most likely be *fear, anxiety, panic, loneliness,* or *despair.*

Now write down the answer to the following question: "What belief might I hold that could create [what you wrote down as your undesirable experience]?"

Continue repeating and answering the question "What *other* belief might I hold that could create [what you wrote down as your undesirable experience]?" until you have a realization—and you will feel it—that you have uncovered the core belief that is creating the undesired experience. In almost all cases, the core belief will be something limiting that you believe about yourself or something you believe about your external world.

Here are some core beliefs from actual exercises:

- "I'm powerless to change my circumstances."

- "I can't do anything, no matter how hard I try."

- "Life will always disappoint me."

- "I can't create what I want."

- "Life's not fair."

Do you see how these limiting beliefs could create fear?

Let's look at "I'm powerless to change my circumstances." This belief might have been created during childhood because of a specific incident. Unfortunately, even in adulthood, it has been turned into a generalized truth. Other beliefs—"I can't do anything, no matter how hard I try," "Life will always disappoint me," "I can't create what I want," "Life's not fair"—all seem to be similar. They are early childhood decisions (beliefs) that have been generalized to apply to *all* situations.

If you were observing someone who expressed these beliefs, what would you say to him or her? My first question would be, "Were you aware that you held that belief?" People usually say no, but immediately begin relating their story about when they created the belief. With a little thought, they realize that the belief they created, many years ago, doesn't apply to every situation, and they can choose to change it. *Choose* is the key word. Beliefs are changed by *choice*. Just *choose* a new one: "I am powerful." "I can create what I want."

If you find limiting beliefs similar to those mentioned above on your Inside Resume, apply the same analysis. Does the belief apply to *all* situations? Is there a different point of view that you can choose? When you arrive at a new, more empowering belief, add it to your Inside Resume. It will provide you with more fulfilling experiences.

This is a very powerful exercise. Changing the limiting belief eliminates a major source of worry, fear, and doubt. Quite often, we feel that we are dealing with worry or fear, but what really is causing the emotional upset is doubt. Doubt arises when you believe that there is something in your life that you can't handle or there is some outcome that you can't control.

There may be additional sources still present on your Inside Resume, so be courageous and apply this technique each time an unwanted emotion arises. Before long, nothing will disturb your peace of mind.

By now, I trust that you understand that you have complete control over how you handle anything in your life. *What you believe will determine how you experience anything that shows up.* We all have control over what we choose to believe. So remember, if you are having an experience that you prefer not to have, review your Inside Resume. It might be time for another revision.

As you move forward with your job search, your Inside Resume needs to contain some of the following beliefs: "I have unique knowledge and skills that are in demand." "I am proud of my accomplishments." "I have the courage to move through fear and doubt." "The perfect job is out there for me." "Look out world, here I come."

As you revise the beliefs on your Inside Resume you will notice that you will *be* different, and *being different* will cause you to *do* more of the things required to *have* what you want. Be, do, have—it's a powerful formula. Use your Inside Resume to make it work for you.

In Part II of "The Inside Resume," you will discover how the Inside Resume contributes to actually creating your outside resume.

Part II

In Part I, we discussed how the content of your Inside Resume—your beliefs—determines how you experience events in your life. We covered the concept of be, do, have, in which your state of *being*—your energetic state—determines what you *do* (or don't do), and what you do (or don't do) determines what you *have* (or don't have). The underlying theme is *the beliefs you hold are the main, driving force behind what you have or don't have in your life*. This being the case, it is vital to understand what's on your Inside Resume, because it impacts your outside resume.

In the previous sections, I described what may be a new concept for you about thought and belief. If it is new for you, just be open to the possibility that what I am saying might have some validity in your life. If it doesn't, let go of it.

To review, the concept states that thoughts are not just quiet notions that appear in your head for you to ponder or use in making decisions. Thoughts are things. They are minute particles of energy that interact with other intelligent information in the Universe. The actual physical thought energy has form and color. It's called a thoughtform. In 1901, C. W. Leadbeater and his associate, Annie Besant, published a book titled *Thought-Forms*. Both Besant and Leadbeater were gifted clairvoyants who could see energy that is invisible to most humans. Their book pictorially illustrates various thoughtforms. Happy thoughts have thoughtforms with friendly shapes and bright colors.

Negative thoughts have thoughtforms with distorted shapes and deep, dark colors.

Because beliefs are thoughts that you have accepted as being your truth, you can see that the same energetic principle applies to beliefs: beliefs are energy forms emanating out into the universe.

We all have an energetic signature, just like our thumbprint that identifies our individual uniqueness. The thoughts that we think and the beliefs that we hold define our unique energy pattern. Did you ever meet people that you never laid eyes on before and felt a very strong attraction to them? You were identifying with their energy pattern. Their energy pattern was probably very similar to yours. Likewise, you have met people with whom you did not feel comfortable. They had a significantly different energy pattern—not wrong, just different.

The mission of a thought or a belief is to fulfill the intent of the thinker or believer. The energy form goes out into the universe to find other thoughts and/or beliefs that are similar. Events, circumstances, and relationships are then created to fulfill the intent of the thought or belief. In other words, the universe provides events, circumstances, and relationships to prove to you that what you believe is true. There are numerous quotes and sayings that refer to this concept:

"That's a self-fulfilling prophecy." "Seek and ye shall find." "Knock and it shall be opened unto you."

I like to use the following analogy to describe the beliefs-determine-experience concept: The universe is like a cosmic computer that receives information from us. We all put our thoughts, beliefs, desires, and wishes—and yes, our prayers—into the Cosmic Computer for fulfillment. The outputs of the Cosmic Computer are the events, circumstances, and relationships that are created in response to the input.

If you are still with me, then you can understand how the beliefs in your Inside Resume not only determine your experience of external events, but are also responsible for *creating* those events.

This concept is difficult for some individuals to accept because it means that each one of us is totally responsible for what we experience as our life. When I was first introduced to this concept, I said to myself, "No way! Why would I have created all those disappointing events in my life?" Well, I can confidently tell you that I did—not knowingly, of course, but by default. When I say "by default," I mean that I had no idea that I was holding certain beliefs in my Inside Resume that were making unconscious requests of the Cosmic Computer on my behalf. The Cosmic Computer is impersonal. It takes the input and just processes it. It doesn't make judgments or ask,

"Does this request make sense?" If you do not have a belief that is contrary to your request, you will get what you request. That is the $1,000,000 secret: *If you do not have a belief that is contrary to your request, you will get your request.* The response from the Cosmic Computer is always yes. Hence the saying, "Watch what you ask for; you are liable to get it."

Unfortunately, most of us have beliefs on our Inside Resume that we are not consciously aware of. These unconscious beliefs are creating circumstances in our lives that we would prefer not to have. The disappointments and accomplishments on your external resume are related to limiting beliefs on your Inside Resume.

Having gotten the message, I have worked diligently over the years to continue to revise my Inside Resume. Believe me when I suggest that reviewing and revising your Inside Resume will pay huge dividends and increase the strength of your outside resume, placing you in a solid position to have what you want and deserve. (*Deserve* is a key word. Do you have limiting beliefs about how much—or how little—you deserve?)

Let's see if I can help you review and possibly make some revisions to your Inside Resume. First of all, we need to see what's presently written on your Inside Resume. The easiest way to do that is to have you write out what you think is there. You now have the opportunity to map the current beliefs on your Inside Resume by completing the following Career-Beliefs Mapping Exercise.

Career-Beliefs Mapping Exercise

Work quickly and write down—in a notebook—the first thoughts that come to mind upon reading each opening phrase. Your thoughts do not have to make sense. Be very honest with yourself; you will achieve greater benefit from the exercise if you are.

My Environment

Life is _____

Work is _____

Three things I would like to change about my
job are _____

Other(s)

Top management is _____

Supervisors are _____

People are _____

Money is _____

Clients/customers are _____

Competitors are _____

Suppliers are _____

Salespeople are _____

Engineers are _____

Finance people are _____

Relationships are _____

You can't trust _____

_____ will betray you every time.

The characteristics that one of my coworkers has that bug me the most are _____

My Self

Expressing feelings at work is _____

My career would be better if only _____

When I make mistakes, I _____

I must keep my boss happy. True or False _____

It's important that others like me. True or False

_____

I'm paid what I'm worth. True or False _____

I see myself as someone who is successful. True or False _____

It's _____ for me to ask for what I want.

_____ really makes me angry.

I don't express myself fully at work because _____

I can't _____

I am avoiding telling _____

I am avoiding _____

I _____ get what I want.

When I miss my goals, it's because _____

Regarding my **life:** I am committed to _____

Regarding my **job:** I am committed to _____

Regarding my **finances:** I am _____

Regarding my **coworkers:** I am _____

Regarding my **integrity:** I am _____

Regarding my **personality:** I am _____,
_____, and _____.

Three things I would like to change about myself
are: _____

When my feelings are hurt, I _____

My biggest fear is _____

I am protecting _____

Why? _____

I am afraid of _____

I am afraid to _____

Being right is _____

I make _____ decisions

I will really be happy when _____

What I want is _____

I don't have it because _____

Something else that I want is _____

I don't have it because _____

Another thing that I want is _____

I don't have it because _____

Something that I will *never* have is _____

Why? _____

What would happen if I had it? _____

I would be more successful if only _____

The following thoughts come to mind when I say to myself, "I am glad I'm me." _____

My greatest asset is _____

I am really good at _____

I am the happiest when _____

The thing I love the most about myself is _____

The thing I love most about my life is _____

It really makes me laugh when _____

I am successful because _____

You have just mapped out the script for a movie titled *Your Career.* The career that you are experiencing is a direct reflection of what you just defined for your Inside Resume. Your career is documented on your traditional outside resume—the paper one. The accomplishments will link to the empowering beliefs on your Inside Resume, and the shortfalls will be linked to the limiting beliefs on your Inside Resume. Let's examine a few possibilities and see if I can get you to see a pattern.

What was your answer to "Life is"? Was it empowering or limiting? Empowering beliefs such as "Life is great," "Life is an opportunity," "Life is exciting," and "Life is a gift" would provide you with positive experiences, and great success would show up on your resume. Limiting beliefs such as "Life is a struggle," "Life is tough," "Life is not fair," and "Life is difficult" are limiting beliefs and would show up on your resume as missed goals, job loss, and conflict with others. What do you notice about your response and your experiences?

What are your responses to "Money is" and "I am paid what I am worth"? Are they empowering you, or are you limiting yourself?

What is it that you want in your life, but will *never* have? What have you told yourself is the reason you won't have it? Your reason is a limiting belief.

What is it that you are afraid to say? To whom? What is it that you are afraid to do? What is it that you can't do?

The answers to all of these questions are limiting beliefs that have you feeling stuck not only in your job search, but also in your life. Are the beliefs really true? Did you create these limiting beliefs based on some experience years ago and find that you have generalized the belief to apply to *all* similar situations?

Change your Inside Resume to remove the limiting beliefs that are impacting your outside resume. These changes are made by *choice*. Once you are aware of the limiting beliefs, simply decide to replace them with empowering ones and update your Inside Resume. Then the next time you update your outside resume, you will see less misfortune and more accomplishments. The accomplishments will come with less effort because you will not have to use brute force to overcome the limitations. Your accomplishments will come easily and effortlessly. (That's a good belief for your Inside Resume: "My accomplishments come easily and effortlessly.")

Do yourself a big favor and review the rest of the beliefs on your Inside Resume. Make a conscious effort to identify the limiting beliefs, evaluate them, and change them to update your Inside Resume. Your next employer will see a very powerful resume filled with great accomplishments. The reflection from your Inside Resume will be quite obvious, and the rewards will be well worth it. Go for it!

General Beliefs Mapping Exercise

After exploring your beliefs about your career or work, you probably can see how to map out the beliefs about other areas of life. Completing the phrases in the following General Beliefs Mapping Exercise will shed light on your unconscious beliefs. From there, you can decide which beliefs are serving you well and which you want to change.

I suggest writing your answers to the phrases in a notebook for future reference. They will give you excellent benchmarks from which to witness your progress.

Phrase Completion

Write as many endings as you can, as quickly as you can, for the "I am" phrases in each category. Let your mind free flow. Your answers don't have to be logical or make sense.

Physically, I am _____

Emotionally, I am _____

Mentally, I am _____

Socially, I am _____

In my career, I am _____

In relationships, I am _____

When it comes to love, I am _____

When it comes to family, I am _____

Similarly, complete as many phrases as you can for the following:

_____ makes me feel happy.

_____ makes me feel sad.

_____ makes me feel angry.

_____ makes me feel guilty.

Men are _____

Women are _____

Babies are _____

Puppies are _____

Money is _____

People are _____

Sex is _____

Life is _____

Love is _____

I am a person who _____

I can _____

I can't _____

I should _____

I shouldn't _____

It's wrong to _____

I am too _____

I _____ myself.

After you have completed the exercise, make a note beside each of your responses for empowering beliefs (E) and for limiting beliefs (L). Quite revealing, isn't it? How many of these limiting beliefs would you like to eliminate?

Reflection

Select an item from your list of things that bother you—one that has a great deal of emotional charge attached to it. Something that really disturbs you. Write in your notebook your answers to the following questions about the item you selected.

1. When you noticed unpleasant feelings, what did you believe was happening?

2. Can you think of another belief that may also be valid in this situation?

3. How many other beliefs can you think of?

4. Seeing that there are other beliefs (perspectives), can you now let go of the original belief that you had, knowing that it's only one perspective of many?

Here's an example. Situation: "Every time someone goes into my boss's office and closes the door, I feel uneasy."

1. When you noticed unpleasant feelings, what did you believe was happening?

   "I felt as though they were talking about me."

2. Can you think of another belief that may also be valid in this situation?

   "They may have been talking about someone else."

3. How many other beliefs can you think of?

"They may not have been talking about anyone else. They may have been discussing my coworker's performance. They may have been working out a schedule. My coworker may have just had a question about a work assignment."

4. Seeing that there are other beliefs (perspectives), can you now let go of the original belief that you had, knowing that it's only one perspective of many?

"Gosh, how silly of me to assume that just because the door is closed, my boss and my coworker are talking about me. There are many things they could have been discussing. You know, it reminds me of when I was young. When my dad would come home from work, he and my mother would talk in their bedroom behind closed doors while he was changing his clothes. If she reported that I had misbehaved during the day, he would whip me. I guess when people are talking behind closed doors at the office, it seems the same. From now on, I sure won't assume that people are talking about me when their door is closed. That's ridiculous."

Bringing the situation to this new level of awareness will often resolve the issue.

Summary Points for Reflection

Thoughts exist as thoughtforms.

Thoughts generate feelings.

Thoughtforms exist to fulfill their intent.

Thoughtforms attract similar thoughtforms.

Thoughts that I accept as true become my beliefs.

Beliefs are specialized thoughtforms.

My beliefs determine my experiences.

The sum of my beliefs makes up my individual belief system.

My individual belief system generates my energetic signature.

My energetic signature attracts my life's circumstances.

Beliefs are empowering or limiting.

Limiting beliefs inhibit the expression of my true self.

What I focus my attention on expands in my life.

Attention strengthens thoughtforms.

I will keep my attention focused on my goals.

Self-responsibility creates inner power.

My external events (experiences) are determined by my internal events (beliefs).

The universe mirrors my beliefs back to me.

Judgments, fear, worry, and doubt are all tied to limiting beliefs.

A positive attitude attracts positive circumstances.

Experiencing is feeling.

I can only experience in the present moment—*now*.

I experience my beliefs about the past—not the past itself.

Limiting beliefs negate my desires.

Old limiting beliefs become weaker when challenged.

Beliefs are added and removed by choice.

I stay positive.

I believe in myself.

I increase my self-awareness.

I remove the limiting thoughtforms that I choose to remove.

I create what I want.

I love myself.

The accumulation of all of my individual beliefs makes up my belief system.

Belief precedes experience.

My energetic signature attracts my life's circumstances.

Everyone has his or her own truth.

What I focus on expands in my life.

Judgments are tied to beliefs.

I dissolve old limiting beliefs.

YOUR BELIEF SYSTEM

The mechanism that Is the foundation of your experience

Thoughts and Beliefs ⟹ **Experience**

- Your **Belief System** is the "cause"—**thoughts** are the "effect."

- Your **Belief System** provides the **"Blue Print"** for your life **experiences**.

- To change your thinking, you must change your **Belief System**.

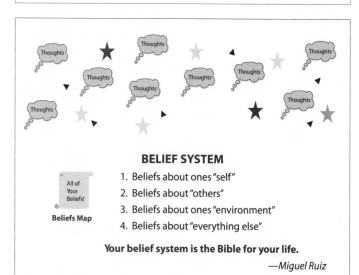

BELIEF SYSTEM

All of Your Beliefs!

Beliefs Map

1. Beliefs about ones "self"

2. Beliefs about "others"

3. Beliefs about ones "environment"

4. Beliefs about "everything else"

Your belief system is the Bible for your life.

—*Miguel Ruiz*

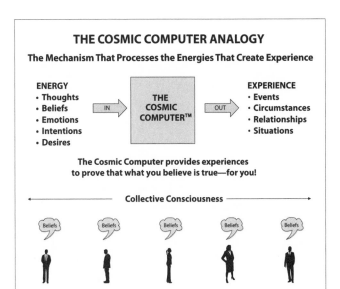

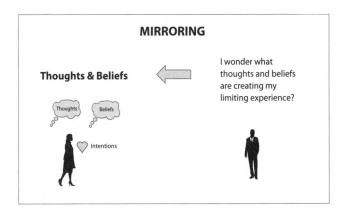

Go Exploring

It is my hope that the information you have just read will entice you to continue exploring how your thoughts and your beliefs impact your life's experience. I suggest that you frequently refer to the General Beliefs Mapping Exercise to remind you to explore and remove your limiting beliefs.

My wish is for every person on the planet—especially our young people—to have some insight into the fundamentals of thought and the power that we all have at our disposal to design our lives deliberately. We all have the innate ability to create anything that we can imagine. The holographic universe is energetically structured to turn every desire into reality if that desire is not impaired by a previously created conflicting belief. By removing your limiting beliefs, you will accelerate the opportunity to *think your way to the life you want*.

My challenge to you is this: never give up if you believe in something—especially if it's yourself!

Many blessings!

About the Author

Bruce I. Doyle III, Ph.D., has over twenty-five years of experience as a corporate executive and business consultant focused on organizational and individual transformation. He is recognized as an inspirational leader who creates transformation based on his philosophy, "Lead the People—Manage

the Business!" This philosophy embraces the value of leading from the heart to create an environment that fosters integrity and open, honest relationships to facilitate the mutual achievement of both individual and corporate goals.

He holds B.S. and M.S. degrees in electrical engineering from Penn State University and Virginia Polytechnic Institute. His Ph.D. is

Photo credit: Visual Photography

146

in organizational development and transformation from the International University of Professional Studies. He enjoys flying and is an instrument-rated private pilot. Dr. Doyle is dedicated to helping individuals achieve their full potential through the realization that their beliefs create their life experiences.

Hampton Roads Publishing Company

. . . for the evolving human spirit

HAMPTON ROADS PUBLISHING COMPANY
publishes books on a variety of subjects, including
spirituality, health, and other related topics.

For a copy of our latest trade catalog,
call 978-465-0504 or
visit our website at *www.hrpub.com*